Food Preparation and Cooking

Student Guide

Core Units

The complete material for Food Preparation and Cooking consists of three books:

Student Guide: *Core Units*
Student Guide: *Cookery Units*
Tutor Resource Pack

Catering and Hospitality

NVQ Level 2

Food Preparation and Cooking

Student Guide
Core Units

Ann Bulleid, Malcolm Ware, Philip Coulthard,
Roland Foote, David Klaasen

First published in 1993 by:
Stanley Thornes (Publishers) Ltd
Ellenborough House
Wellington Street
Cheltenham
Gloucestershire GL50 1YD
England

The catalogue record for this book
is available from The British Library.
ISBN 0-7487-1603-3

Reprinted 1993

The authors and publishers would like to thank Andy Armiger, Bill Moorcroft, Andy Robertson and Tony Groves for their help and advice. They would also like to thank the following for permission to reproduce photographs: Lockhart Catering Equipment (pp. 36, 101, 103, 105, 109, 113), Lever Industrial (p. 100), Roland Foote (pp. 54, 55, 59, 62, 67, 68, 69, 71, 73, 83, 88, 90, 91, 92, 93), Andrew Nisbet and Co Ltd (pp. 45, 46).

Typeset by The New Leaf Book Company, Oxford
Printed and bound in Great Britain at Scotprint, Musselburgh

Contents

UNIT G1

Maintaining a safe and secure working environment

ELEMENTS 1–5: Carrying out procedures in the event of fire, accident or discovery of suspicious packages. Maintaining a safe and secure environment

What do you have to do?

- Take account of customers', staff and visitors' reactions when involved with emergencies and deal with them accordingly.
- Identify hazards or potential hazards and take appropriate action to deal with the situation.
- Identify all company procedures for dealing with emergency situations.
- Comply with all relevant health and safety legislation.
- Ensure that safety and security procedures and practices are followed at all times in a calm, orderly manner.

What do you need to know?

- What action to take when dealing with an emergency situation such as fire, accident or the discovery of a suspicious item or package.
- Why suspicious items or packages should never be approached or tampered with.
- Why suspicious items or packages must always be reported immediately.
- Why keys, property and storage areas should be secured from unauthorised access at all times.
- How to identify and deal with safety hazards or potential safety hazards for customers, staff and visitors.
- Why preventative action must always be taken quickly when a potential hazard is spotted.
- What action to take when challenging suspicious individuals.
- Who to contact in the event of an emergency and the information they will need.
- The procedures for ensuring the security of the establishment and property within it.
- Why and what preventative actions are needed to maintain a safe environment.
- What action to take when establishment, customer or staff property is reported missing.

ELEMENT 1: Carrying out procedures in the event of a fire

Introduction

Fires occur each week on premises where staff are working and customers or visitors are present. Many, fortunately, are quite small and can be dealt with quickly. Others lead to tragic loss of life, personal injury and devastation of property.

Some of these fires could have been prevented with a little forethought, care and organisation. The commonest causes are misuse of electrical or heating equipment, and carelessly discarded cigarette-ends. People are often the link needed to start a fire: by acting negligently, perhaps by leaving rubbish in a dark corner; or by being lazy and taking shortcuts in work methods.

Fire hazards

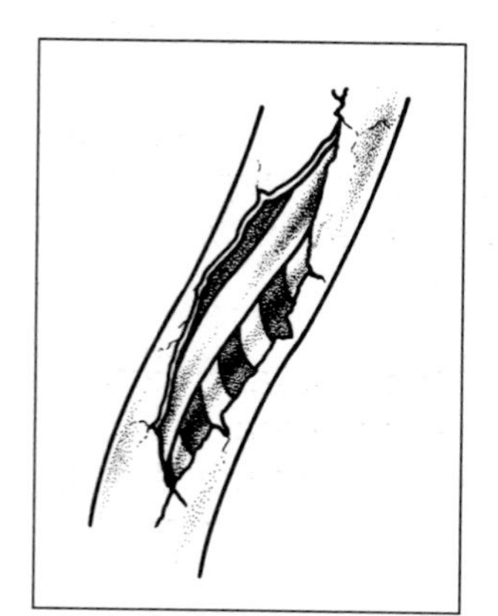

Damaged wiring

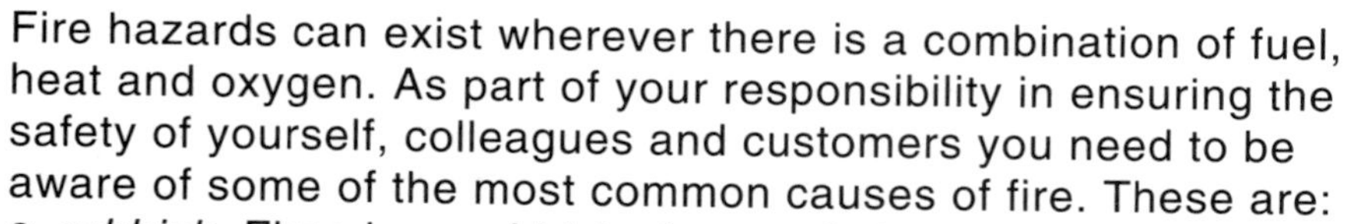

Fire hazards can exist wherever there is a combination of fuel, heat and oxygen. As part of your responsibility in ensuring the safety of yourself, colleagues and customers you need to be aware of some of the most common causes of fire. These are:

- *rubbish.* Fires love rubbish. Accumulations of cartons, packing materials and other combustible waste products are all potential flashpoints
- *electricity.* Although you cannot see it, the current running through your electric wiring is a source of heat and, if a fault develops in the wiring, that heat can easily become excessive and start a fire. Neglect and misuse of wiring and electrical appliances are the leading causes of fires in business premises
- *smoking.* The discarded cigarette end is still one of the most frequent fire starters. Disposing of waste correctly will help reduce fires from this source, but even so, remember that wherever cigarettes and matches are used there is a chance of a fire starting
- *flammable goods.* If items such as paint, adhesives, oil or chemicals are stored or used on your premises they should be kept in a separate store room and well away from any source of heat. Aerosols, gas cartridges and cylinders, if exposed to heat, can explode and start fires
- *heaters.* Portable heaters, such as the sort used in restaurants and offices to supplement the general heating, can be the cause of a fire if goods come into close contact with them or if they are accidentally knocked over. Never place books, papers or clothes over convector or storage heaters, as this can cause them to overheat and can result in a fire.

Fire legislation

The Fire Precautions Act 1971 requires companies to comply with certain legal conditions, such as those listed on the next page:

- providing a suitable means of escape, which is unlocked, unobstructed, working and available whenever people are in the building
- ensuring suitable fire fighting equipment is properly maintained and readily available
- meeting the necessary requirements for a fire certificate. On larger premises, where more than twenty people are employed, the owners are required to have a fire certificate which regulates the means of escape and markings of fire exits. These premises must also have properly maintained fire alarms and employees must be made aware of the means of escape and the routine to follow in the event of a fire
- posting relevant emergency signs around the area giving people guidance on what to do in the event of a fire and where to go.

Preventing fires

Being alert to the potential hazard of fire can help prevent emergencies. Potential fire hazards exist in every area of the workplace, so regular preventative checks are essential as part of your everyday working practice.

- As far as possible, switch off and unplug all electrical equipment when it is not being used. Some equipment may be designed to be permanently connected to the mains (e.g. video recorders with digital clocks); always check the manufacturer's instructions.
- If new equipment is being installed, ensure this is carried out properly and arrange a system of regular maintenance.
- Electrical equipment is covered by British Safety Standards, so look for plugs that conform to BS1363 and fuses that conform to BS1362.
- Ensure there are sufficient ash trays available for smokers to use.
- Inspect all public rooms, kitchens, staff rooms and store rooms to ensure all discarded smoking equipment is collected in lidded metal bins and not mixed with other waste.
- As often as possible, look behind cushions and down the side of seats to check a cigarette end has not been dropped by mistake. You could check for this whenever you are tidying cushions, or after guests have left an area.
- Ensure rooms and corridors are free of waste and rubbish, especially in areas where litter tends to collect, such as in corners and underneath stairwells.
- Place all accumulated waste in appropriate receptacles, away from the main building.
- Check that all external stairways and means of escape are kept clear.
- Make sure that fire doors and smoke stop doors on escape routes are regularly maintained. These doors are designed to withstand heat and to reduce the risks from smoke. They must not be wedged open or prevented from working properly in the event of a fire.

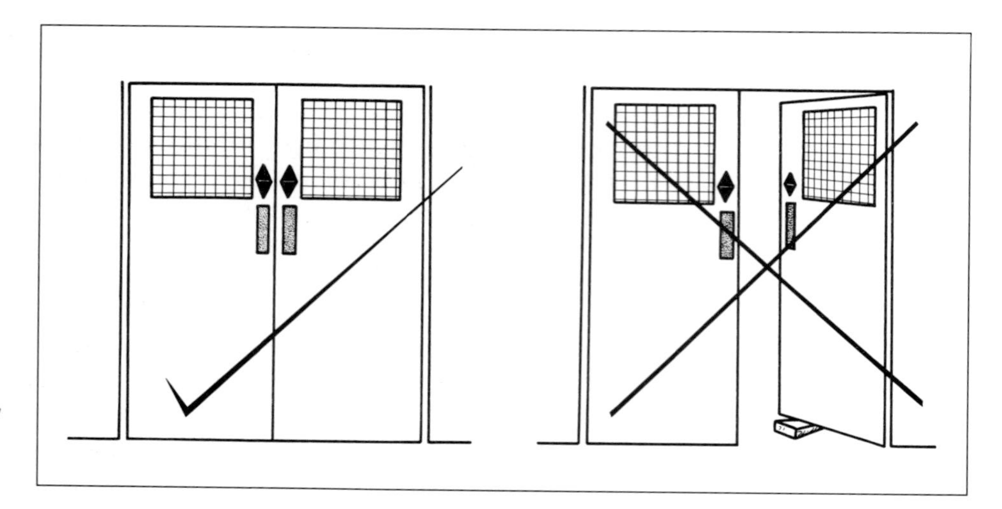

Fire doors used correctly (left) and incorrectly (right)

In the kitchen and restaurant

Fire hazards

In a kitchen or restaurant there are additional hazards that you should be aware of. These areas, the kitchen in particular, tend to get hot and fires can easily start. Note the following points.

- Frying operations should be kept under constant supervision.
- Electrical cooking equipment (e.g. deep fat fryers) with faulty controls or thermostats can cause any oil or fat being used to overheat, ignite and cause a fire. All equipment must be maintained and kept free from build-up of grease or dirt. Check that extraction hoods and grease traps are cleaned and maintained regularly (see Unit 2D12, pages 99–110).
- Cloths, aprons and loose clothing should be kept away from any open flames on a stove. It is very easy for fabric to catch alight and cause a fire to spread.
- Gas cylinders, used perhaps in the restaurant, should be in good condition and undamaged. Staff using the cylinders must be thoroughly trained in their use and aware of dangers from inadequate storage and damage to the cylinders.

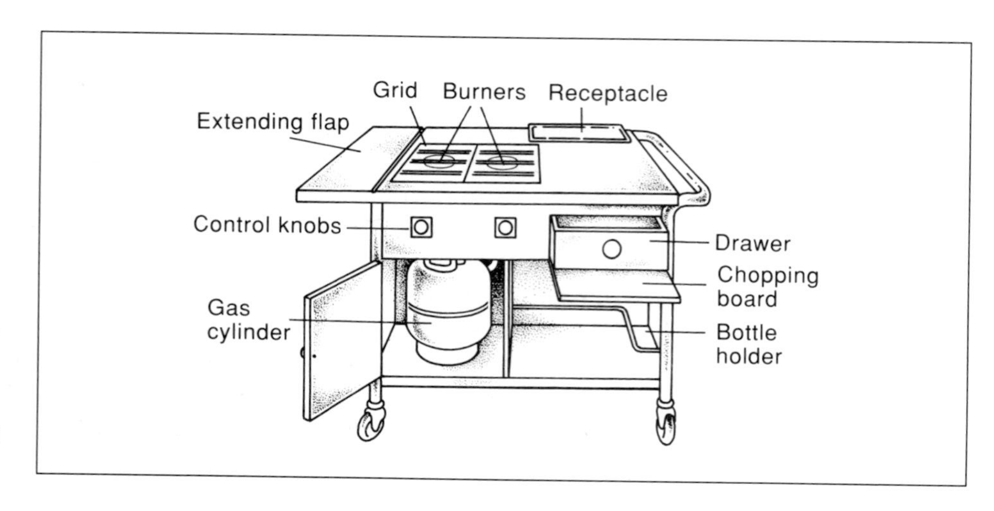

Gueridon trolley showing gas cylinder in place

- Any CO_2 cylinders in cellars must be properly secured and free from damage.
- If candles are used in the restaurant, care must be taken to ensure they are kept away from flammable material.
- If there is an open fire in the restaurant, customers, visitors and staff must be protected from the flames by a fire guard.

Fire safety conditions

The following conditions must always be met within a working area.

- Fire doors should not be hooked or wedged open (see illustration opposite). Check that they close automatically when released. Fire stop doors held by magnets need to be closed from 11 p.m.–7 a.m.
- Fire extinguishers should be available, full and not damaged.
- Fire exit doors should be easy to use and secure.
- Emergency lighting should be maintained and visible at all times. Make sure that the lights are not obscured by screens, drapes, clothing, etc.
- Signs and fire notices giving details of exit routes must be available in all areas and kept in good condition.
- Alarm points should be readily accessible and free from obstruction.
- Fire sprinklers and smoke detectors must be kept clear of obstruction for at least 24 inches in all directions.
- Fire exit doors and routes must be kept clear at all times and in a good state of repair.

To do

- Carry out a full survey of your own work area and identify any potential fire hazards. List the hazards under the following categories: combustible material, flammable liquids, flammable gases, electrical hazards.
- Discuss the potential dangers with your colleagues and agree ways of minimising the risk.
- Revise your own working methods to minimise fire risks.

Discovering a fire

If you discover a fire, follow the sequence of events given below:

1. sound the alarm immediately
2. call the fire brigade
3. evacuate the area
4. assemble in the designated safe area for roll call.

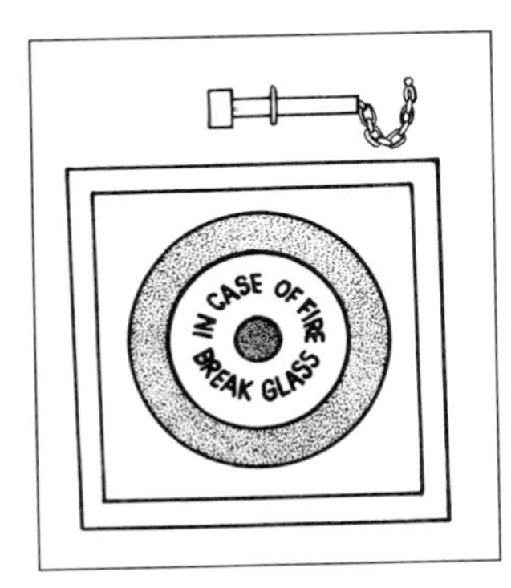

A break glass alarm

Sounding the alarm

The function of the alarm is to warn every person in the building that an emergency has arisen and that fire evacuation procedures may need to be put into action. Most alarms are known as *break glass* alarms, and, as the name suggests, you have to break the glass to make the alarm sound.

Calling the fire brigade

The responsibility for calling the fire brigade falls to different people in different establishments. Often it is a receptionist or telephonist who will be expected to deal with the call. Make sure that you know who is responsible for this in your establishment.

When calling the fire brigade, be ready with the following information:

- your establishment's address
- your establishment's telephone number
- the precise location of the fire.

You may like to write down the necessary information about the establishment and keep it near the telephone in case of an emergency. If you do have to make an emergency phone call, make sure that you listen for the address to be repeated back to you before replacing the telephone receiver.

Evacuating the area and assembling outside

It is essential for everyone to be able to escape from danger. If you do not have specific duties to carry out in the evacuation procedures you should leave the premises immediately on hearing the alarm.

When evacuating the premises:

- switch off equipment and machinery
- close windows and doors behind you
- follow marked escape routes
- remain calm, do not run
- assist others in their escape
- go immediately to an allocated assembly point
- do not return for belongings, no matter how valuable.

You and all of your colleagues should be instructed on what to do if fire breaks out. Customers and visitors should also be made aware of what to do in the event of a fire and made familiar with the means of escape provided. This is usually done by means of notices in all public areas and rooms. Where accommodation is provided for foreign guests, notices should be printed in the most appropriate languages.

Fighting fires

Fighting fires can be a dangerous activity, and is generally to be discouraged. Personal safety and safe evacuation must always be your primary concern. If a fire does break out, it should only be tackled in its very early stages and before it has started to spread.

Before you tackle a fire:

- evacuate everyone and follow the emergency procedure to alert the fire brigade. Tell someone that you are attempting to tackle the fire

- always put your own and other people's safety first; never risk injury to fight fires. Always make sure you can escape if you need to and remember that smoke can kill. Remember the rule: *if in doubt, get out*
- never let a fire get between you and the way out. If you have any doubt about whether the extinguisher is suitable for the fire do not use it; leave immediately
- remember that fire extinguishers are only for 'first aid' fire fighting. Never attempt to tackle the fire if it is beginning to spread or if the room is filling with smoke
- if you cannot put out the fire, or your extinguisher runs out, leave immediately, closing doors and windows as you go.

Fire fighting equipment

Types

On-premise fire fighting equipment is designed to be used for small fires only and is very specific to the type of fire. Hand extinguishers are designed to be easy to use, but can require practice and training in how to use them.

All fire fighting equipment is designed to remove one of the three factors needed for a fire: heat, oxygen or flammable material. Fire extinguishers are filled with one of the following:

- *water*. This type of extinguisher provides a powerful and efficient means of putting out fires involving wood, paper and fabric
- *dry powder*. These extinguishers can be used to put out wood, paper, fabric and flammable liquid fires, but are more generally used for fires involving electrical equipment
- *foam*. The pre-mix foam extinguishers use a combination of water and aqueous film, and are effective for extinguishing paper, wood, fabric and flammable liquid fires
- *carbon dioxide*. These extinguishers are not commonly in use, but can be used in situations where there are flammable oils and spirits, and in offices where there is electronic equipment.

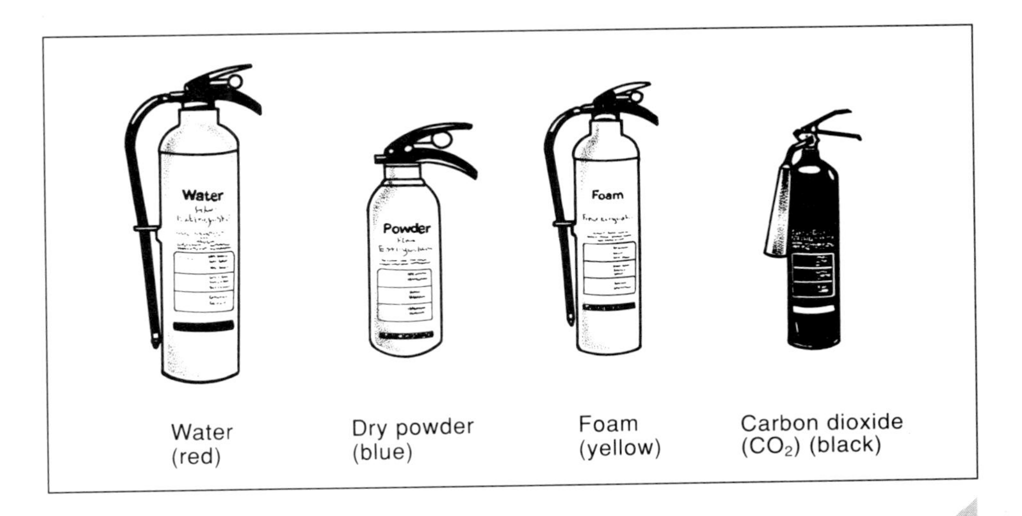

Fire extinguishers

Fire blankets are also used to extinguish fires. These are made from a variety of materials: some are made of woven fibreglass while others have a fibreglass base and are coated with silicone rubber on both sides. Fire blankets are generally housed in a wall-mounted plastic pack with a quick-pull front opening.

Maintaining equipment

Fire fighting equipment is essential in areas where there is a potential risk from fires. It is essential that equipment is:

- *maintained regularly and kept in good condition.* The fire brigade or your supplier will carry out annual checks and note on the extinguisher when the check was carried out
- *kept clear from obstruction at all times.* The equipment must be visible and readily available. Obstructions can prevent easy access and may result in unnecessary damage to the equipment
- *available in all areas of work.* Different types of extinguishers are needed for different fires, so the most suitable extinguisher should be available in the area. Guidance can be sought from the fire brigade or equipment suppliers
- *used by trained operators.* Fire extinguishers can be quite noisy and powerful and can startle you if you have not used one before. It is important that the user knows the best way of utilising the extinguisher to tackle a fire in the most effective way.

How to use a fire blanket

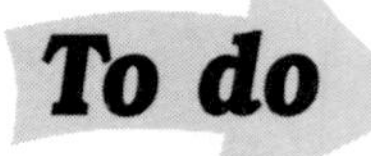

- Find out where your nearest fire exits are located and the route you need to follow to reach your nominated assembly point.
- Identify the fire extinguishers available in your area and learn how to use them.
- Look out for potential fire hazards in your area and remove or report them immediately.
- Take part in practice fire drills in your establishment and learn to recognise the type of sound made by the alarm in your building.

What have you learned?

1 What are the four most common types of fire extinguisher?

Water (red) Dry Powder (blue) Foam (yellow)

CO2 (black

2 What is the first thing you should do on discovering a fire?

3 What type of extinguisher would you use for putting out:

- An electical fire?

- A fire in a deep fat fryer?

- A fire in a store room where chemicals are stored?

4 List four points you need to remember when evacuating your department if the fire alarm sounds.

5 How can you ensure that fire fighting equipment is ready to use whenever you need it?

6 How does a fire blanket work in preventing a fire from spreading?

____

____

7 Why should fire escapes and exits be kept free from rubbish and doors unlocked when people are on the premises?

____

____

ELEMENT 2: Carrying out procedures on discovery of a suspicious item or package

Introduction

In any area of work there may be times when an unattended item, package or bag raises suspicion. This could lead to an emergency, and, if not handled correctly, may result in danger or injury to people in the area.

In recent years there has been an increase in the number of bombs and incendiary devices used by terrorists in pursuit of their particular cause. Evacuations, or closure of shops, transport systems and public areas are no longer an unusual occurrence, especially in large cities. Often these evacuations occur as a result of a hoax, and, although no explosion or fire takes place, businesses often suffer significant damage through the loss of income or delays caused by the need for an evacuation.

It is important to treat any suspicious item seriously. Be aware of the dangers it potentially contains and be prepared to inform people of your suspicions quickly and calmly.

A suspicious package which is not dealt with immediately may result in serious injury to people in the area or serious damage to the building. It is an essential part of your daily work to keep alert to dangers from suspect packages and follow laid down procedures when dealing with the problem.

Recognising a suspicious item or package

It is difficult to give precise guidance about where you may discover a suspicious package, or what size or shape it might be. Either of the types of package listed on the next page might raise your suspicions.

- Something that has been left unattended for some time, such as a briefcase next to a chair, or a suitcase left in a reception area.
- Something that looks out of place, like a man's holdall in the ladies' cloakroom, or a full carrier bag near a rubbish bin.

A full carrier bag left next to an empty rubbish bin might be enough to arouse suspicions

In fact, anything that sticks out in your mind as somewhat unusual.

On discovering a suspicious item

- Do not attempt to move or touch the item. The action of moving or disturbing the item may be enough to start off a reaction leading to an explosion or fire.
- Remain calm and composed. Try not to cause panic by shouting an alarm or running from the item. People and property can be injured through a disorderly or panicked evacuation.
- Report the matter to your supervisor or the police immediately. Check your establishment's procedures to find out who you should inform.
- If possible, cordon off the area and move people away. It may be difficult to do this without causing people in the area to panic, but it is essential that no one attempts to move or touch the item, so you will need to warn people to keep clear.
- At some point it may be necessary to evacuate the building, or the part of the building nearest to the suspect package. This may be a decision taken by your supervisor, or the police if they are involved. If it is thought necessary to clear the area, follow your company procedures for the evacuation of the building.

Essential knowledge

- Suspicious items or packages must never be approached or tampered with in case they contain explosive materials which may be set off.
- Suspicious items or packages must always be reported immediately, to prevent serious accidents occurring involving bombs and explosives.

Reporting a suspicious item

If you are reporting a suspicious item make sure you are able to tell your contact:

1 what the suspicious package looks like:

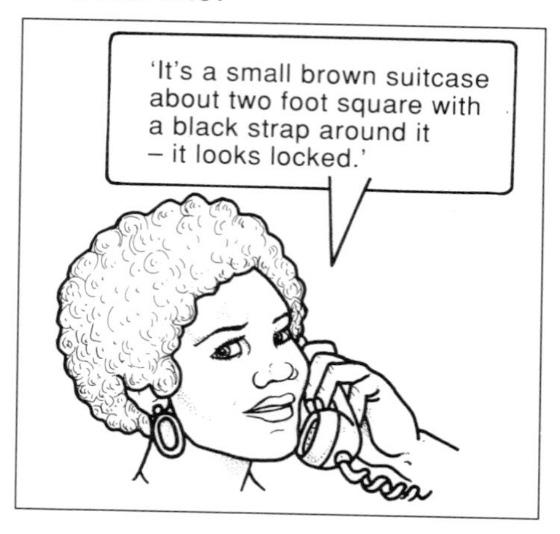

2 the exact location of the suspect device:

3 the precautions you have taken so far:

4 the existence of any known hazards in the surrounding area, e.g. gas points:

5 the reason for your suspicion:

6 any witnesses to the placing of the package or item:

The term was first used in 1894 by the voluntary First Aid organisations and certificates are now offered by St John's Ambulance, St Andrew's Ambulance Association and the British Red Cross. The certificate is only valid for three years, to ensure that first aiders are highly trained, regularly examined and kept up to date in their knowledge and skills.

First Aid organisations (left to right): St John's Ambulance, St Andrew's Ambulance, British Red Cross

Once the first aider is dealing with the casualty their main aims are to:

- preserve life
- prevent the condition worsening
- promote recovery.

Their responsibility is to:

- assess the situation
- carry out diagnosis of the casualty
- give immediate, appropriate and adequate treatment
- arrange, without delay, for the casualty to be taken to a hospital or to see a doctor if appropriate.

Giving information to the first aider

Once the first aider arrives at the accident they will need certain information from you before they begin their treatment.

Be prepared to tell them as much as you know about:

- *the history of the accident.* How the accident happened, whether the person has been moved, what caused the injury
- *the symptoms.* Where the casualty is feeling pain, what other signs you have observed, whether the symptoms have changed
- *the treatment given.* What has already been done to the casualty and whether the casualty has any other illness or is receiving treatment or medication to the best of your knowledge.

Initial response to an accident

Whether you are a first aider or not, in the event of an accident it is the initial response to the situation and the way laid down procedures are followed that can make the difference to the treatment received by the injured person.

You need to know what immediate response you should give if a person near you sustains an injury. Many of the points are common sense, and will depend upon the extent of the accident and the speed with which you can contact the relevant people.

When dealing with accidents the following points are important.

- *Remain calm when approaching the injured person.* The injured person will probably be frightened by the situation they are in, or may be in pain, and they will benefit from someone taking control of the situation. This may help reduce the feeling of panic, helplessness or embarrassment they may be experiencing.
- *Offer reassurance and comfort.* Keep the casualty (if conscious) informed of the actions you are taking by talking in a quiet, confident manner. Do not move the person but keep them warm, covering them with a blanket, or a coat if necessary. By keeping them warm you are minimising the risk of shock which can often cause the condition of the injured person to deteriorate. By preventing them from moving you are allowing time for them to recover and reducing the possibility of further injury.
- *Do not give them anything to drink.* If the casualty is given something to drink they may not be able to have an anaesthetic if necessary. A drink may also make them feel worse and may cause nausea.
- *Contact or instruct someone else to contact a first aider.*
- *Stay by the casualty* if you can, to reassure them and ensure they do not cause further injury to themselves.
- *Minimise the risk of danger* to yourself, the injured person and any other people in the area.

In the case of:

1. *gas or poisonous fumes:* if possible, cut off the source.
2. *electrical contact:* break the contact either by removing the injured person from the source, or removing the source. Do this by using something that does not conduct electricity, such as a wooden broom handle. Make sure that you do not come into contact with the electrical source yourself. Take precautions against further contact.
3. *fire, or collapsing buildings:* move the casualty to a safe area after temporarily immobilising the injured part of the person.

To do

- Find out the name and work location of your nearest first aider (a list should be displayed in your work area).
- Find out how you can acquire training in First Aid.

Contacting the emergency services

If you or your supervisor decide that assistance is required from the emergency services, or you have been asked to call them by the first aider you will need to pass on certain information:

1. *your telephone number*, so that if for any reason you are cut off, the officer will then be able to contact you

2 *the exact location of the incident.* This will help the ambulance or doctor to get to the scene of the accident more quickly
3 *an indication of the type and seriousness of the accident.* This will allow the team to bring the most appropriate equipment and call for back-up if necessary
4 *the number, sex and approximate age of the casualties involved.* If possible, you should also explain the nature of their injuries
5 *any special help you feel is needed.* For example, in cases where you suspect a heart attack.

It might be a good idea to write down the information you need to pass on before calling the emergency services.

If you do call 999, you will be asked to state the service required: in the case of accidents you would normally state 'ambulance'. The officer responding to your call will be able to pass on messages to any other emergency services necessary, such as gas or fire.

Establishment procedures
Procedures vary from company to company as to who has authority to call the emergency services so it is important that you find out how you are expected to deal with the situation in your own place of work.

Recording an accident

All accidents need to be reported as soon after the event as is practicable. Any accident is required by law to be reported and recorded in an accident book located on the premises. Any accident resulting in serious injury must be reported to the Health and Safety Executive within three working days. Your establishment should have procedures for dealing with this.

In the case of an accident to a member of staff, ideally the person who received the injury would complete the accident book. However, it may be necessary for an appointed person to report the accident on their behalf.

The following information is mandatory:
1 the date and time of the accident
2 the particulars of the person affected:
- full name
- occupation
- nature of injury or condition

3 where the accident happened
4 a brief description of the circumstances.

If an accident happens to a customer or visitor there will probably be different records available. Check on the type of records kept by your own establishment.

Accident record keeping is important, not only to comply with the legal requirements under health and safety legislation, but also to ensure details are available for possible insurance claims. Accident reporting can also be a great help when analysing trends and identifying where there may be a need for preventative training.

To do

- Establish where the Accident Recording Book is located.
- Find out whether there are different procedures and records for accidents involving customers and visitors to those involving staff for your establishment.
- Find out the procedure for reporting accidents to the emergency services.

What have you learned?

1 Why is it important that you deal with an accident quickly?

2 State three things you should remember when dealing with an accident.

3 Why is it important that you remain calm when approaching an injured person?

4 Why should you not attempt to move a person if they have sustained an injury?

ELEMENT 4: Maintaining a safe environment for customers, staff and visitors

Introduction

The safety of everyone who works or visits the premises should be foremost in your mind if accidents are to be prevented and the wellbeing of the business assured.

Under the *Health and Safety at Work Act* (HASAWA,1974) there are certain responsibilities both employers and employees must comply with. Those given below are ones you should be particularly aware of.

Employers' responsibilities
Employers must, as far as is reasonably practicable:

- provide and maintain plants and systems of work that are safe and without risks to health
- make arrangements to ensure safety and the absence of risks to health in connection with the use, handling, storage and transport of articles and substances
- provide such information, instruction, training and supervision as will ensure the health and safety of employees
- maintain any place of work under their control in a safe condition without risks to health and provide at least statutory welfare facilities and arrangements.

These duties also extend to include customers and others visiting the premises.

Employees' responsibilities
As an employee you also have responsibilities and must:

- take reasonable care of your own health and safety
- take reasonable care for the health and safety of other people who may be affected by what you do or neglect to do at work
- cooperate with the establishment in the steps it takes to meet its legal duties
- report any physical conditions or systems which you consider unsafe or potentially unsafe to a supervisor.

These responsibilities have been drawn up for the benefit of everyone in the workplace, to ensure that the risk of accident or injury to anyone is minimised through promotion of a thoughtful and considerate approach to work practices.

Many working days can be lost through accidents, which more often than not are caused through carelessness and thoughtlessness. As a result the business suffers reduced productivity and, in serious cases, considerable trading time if forced to close while the premises are made safe.

Under the HASAWA, Health and Safety inspectors (often under the umbrella of the Environmental Health Office) have the authority to place prohibition notices on premises if they persistently fail to meet the standards set by law. This might occur if there were a physical problem in the building or in equipment, or an outbreak of food poisoning caused by poor hygiene practice.

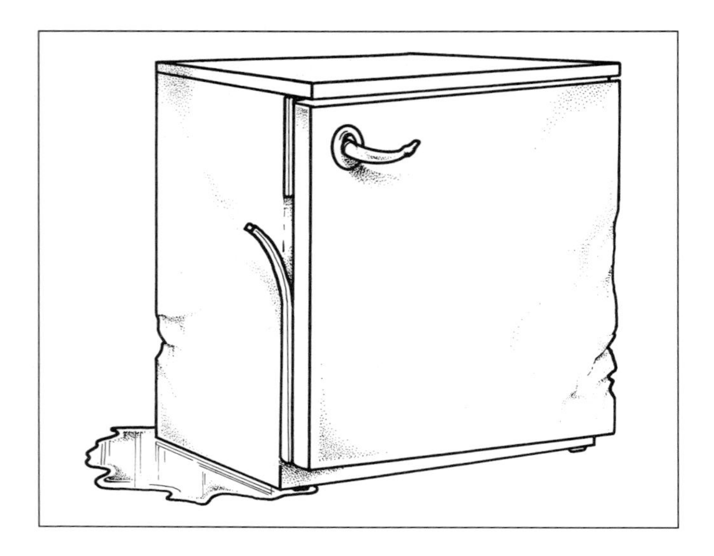

A damaged refrigerator

Whatever the cause, it is important that you and your colleagues have a positive and active approach to maintaining the safety of the environment in which you operate.

The Health and Safety Executive has the responsibility of advising on safety matters and of enforcing the HASAW Act if the obligations of this Act are not met. This is one reason why serious accidents must always be reported to the Executive.

In the case of hotel and catering establishments, Local Authorities appoint their own inspectors: Environmental Health Officers who work with companies and colleges on matters associated with health and safety.

Hazard spotting

Much of the health and safety legislation is aimed at preventing accidents from happening and ensuring the environment is safe for everyone within it. Some of the most common causes of accidents in the workplace are caused through basic mistakes, such as someone not cleaning up a spillage, or a cable left trailing across a walkway.

By being aware of the potential danger of hazards you will be able to contribute effectively to the safety of the area in which you work. The guidelines given on the next page show areas in which you can start contributing towards maintaining a safe environment.

Safety points to remember

- Be constantly aware of obstacles on the floor or in corridors and remove them, returning them to their rightful place.
- Watch out for damaged floor coverings or torn carpets: it is very easy to catch your heel and trip over a carpet edge.
- Make sure electrical cables or wires never run across walkways. Always keep them behind you when you are working to reduce the risk of damage to them.
- Clean up spillages as soon as they occur. If grease is spilt use salt or sand to absorb the spillage before cleaning the area.
- If cleaning up spillages use wet floor signs to warn people of the danger.
- Never handle electrical plugs with wet hands. Water conducts electricity: this can cause death.
- Never use equipment that appears faulty or damaged. You are increasing the risk to yourself by doing so. Report the problem immediately and ensure the equipment is repaired.
- Use a step ladder to reach to the top of shelves. Never stand on piles of cases or boxes.
- If lifting a load, make sure it is not too heavy or awkward for you to move on your own. If you need help, ask. Back injuries are another of the most common reasons for people having to take time out from work.
  The pictures below illustrate the correct way of lifting heavy objects.

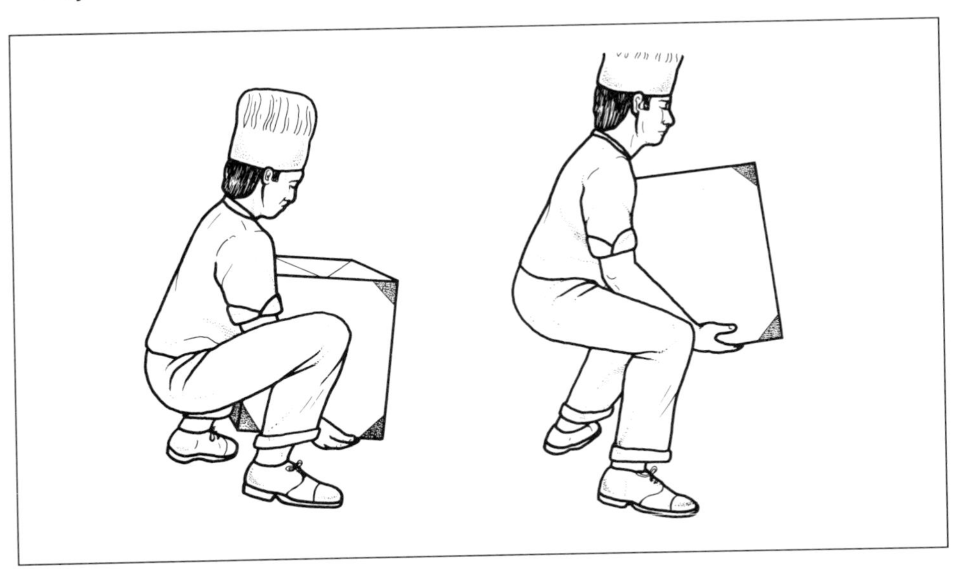

The correct way to lift a heavy object

Kitchen hazards

In the kitchen area there are some special hazards to be aware of. The following points show how these can be kept to a minimum.

- Always use the correct knife for the job you are doing. Use of incorrect knives can lead to accidents. Always leave a knife with its blade flat: if you leave the blade uppermost it would be very easy for you or a colleague to put a hand down on top of the blade and cut the palm of the hand. Never leave a knife immersed in water.

- If walking while carrying knives, always point the blade towards the floor, away from your body. If you were to trip or fall you might end up stabbing someone or injuring yourself. (See also Unit 2D10: *Handling and Maintaining Knives,* pages 42–52.)
- Remember that slicing machines should always be used by trained operators and with the safety guard in place. The machinery must be cleaned by someone over the age of 18. (See also Unit 2D17: *Cleaning cutting equipment,* pages 111–18).
- Always use a dry cloth when handling hot containers as wet cloths can transmit heat and burn you, causing you to drop boiling liquid on yourself.
- Think carefully about how you position pans on the stove. Keep handles away from the heat and do not let them protrude over the edge of the stove where they can easily be knocked off.

Much of the health and safety legislation focuses on people having a thoughtful and commonsense approach to their work and the safety of others. Many of the accidents which happen on premises, whether it be to staff, customers or visitors, occur as a direct result of someone not doing the right thing at the right time.

Sign warning of potential hazard

Preventative action

1 When you spot a hazard, if practicable, remove it immediately and report the situation to your supervisor. Most organisations have a standard Health and Safety Report Form stating action to be taken and follow up procedures. If you are unable to remove the hazard, as in the case of a doorway blocked by a delivery of goods, monitor the situation and if it appears the goods are not to be moved quickly, report the problem to your supervisor. By taking immediate action over a potential hazard you will be contributing to your own wellbeing and that of your colleagues. Some hazards, however, may be due to poor working practices or faulty building design and they will need a different approach and more time to solve.
2 Take note of all signs warning of dangers or potential hazards, especially those associated with:

- use of machinery
- hazardous chemicals
- cleaning fluids.

Essential knowledge

Preventative action should always be taken quickly when a hazard is spotted, in order to

- prevent injury to staff and customers
- prevent damage to buildings and staff
- comply with the law.

Reporting hazards

Under the HASAW Act, every company must have a procedure in place for employees to report potential hazards they have identified. In some companies there may be *Safety Representatives* whose role is to bring the hazard to the supervisor's attention. The Safety Representative may be part of a *Health and Safety Committee* who will meet regularly to deal with matters of safety and to ensure appropriate action is taken.

Your department may have a standard Hazard Report Form which you would complete to help you and your supervisor deal with the hazard through a formalised procedure. You may also be involved in carrying out regular safety audits in your department aimed at ensuring that planned preventative work is implemented.

Under *The Health and Safety at Work Act* it is your responsibility to be aware of potential hazards and to take the necessary action to prevent them from becoming actual hazards.

To do

- Carry out a hazard spotting tour of your area noting any actions needed and highlighting potential dangers.
- Find out how you are required to report health and safety hazards in your place of work.
- Examine the equipment you use in your department. Is the wiring in good condition? When was the equipment last serviced? Discuss any problems found with your supervisor.

What have you learned?

1 Why is it important for you to be aware of the HASAW Act?

____

____

2 What are the main responsibilities for employees under the HASAW Act?

____

____

____

3 What is required of an employer under the HASAW Act?

____

____

____

4 Why is it important to carry out hazard spotting exercises?

____

____

____

____

5 Give three examples of hazards in your workplace.

____

____

____

6 What should you do if you identify something as a hazard and why should action be taken immediately?

____

____

____

____

7 Whose responsibility is it to report hazards?

____

____

ELEMENT 5: Maintaining a secure environment for customers, staff and visitors

Introduction

Maintaining effective security should be the concern of everyone working within an establishment and is an essential part of good business practice. There may be staff within your own organisation employed as *Security Officers* whose role will include all aspects of protecting people on the premises, looking after the security of the building and the property contained within it.

Effective security practices can help protect the profit of the business by reducing the likelihood of losses through, for example:

- *theft,* whether through break-ins causing damage to the building or through walk-outs where customers leave without paying for their service
- *fraud,* by customers or staff
- *missing stock.*

Profitability can be affected both by the immediate loss of property or damage to the building and by bad publicity, which can damage the business through loss of custom.

Your role

Whether or not there are security staff employed within your organisation, you will find there are many situations within your working day where you need to be security conscious. It is easy to become complacent or lazy in your working habits, which can lead to an opportunity being seen and seized by a thief. A common example of this is a member of staff leaving a cash drawer open after transactions for speed or ease of use, allowing a customer to remove cash from the till when the cashier turns away.

Daily work patterns may also present an opportunity to be exploited by a thief. When we work in an area we become familiar with our surroundings, used to seeing things in a certain place and following procedures in a certain way. It is often these patterns that are observed by potential thieves and which can lead to break-ins or thefts.

Being aware of potential breaches of security and knowing how to report them or the action to take is an essential starting point. Think about the way you work and how security conscious you are. Make sure that you always follow the basic security practices listed below.

- Handle all cash transactions away from the customer and preferably out of their sight.
- Keep display materials beyond the reach of any customers and as far away from main entrances as possible, making it difficult for people to remove the items without being spotted.
- Keep security issues and procedures confidential: you can never be sure who might overhear you discussing a sensitive issue.
- Keep your own belongings, such as handbags or wallets, secure and out of sight in a locked compartment or drawer.
- Keep alert to anything or anyone which looks suspicious, for example: an occupied car parked outside the building for a long period of time, boxes or ladders placed near to windows, fire exits left open.
- Keep keys, especially master keys, under close supervision. You will probably find that your establishment has a log book for recording the issue of keys.

It is important for you to follow any particular security procedures that are in place in your establishment. These procedures are often there both for your benefit and to minimise any loss to the business.

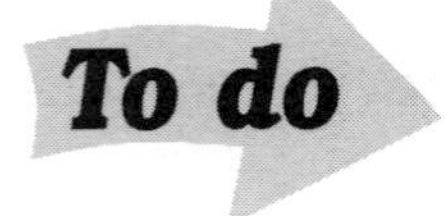

- Think about your working day. List the things you do where attention to security is essential.
- Now write down your ideas for improving security within your job. Discuss your ideas with your supervisor.
- Find out what security procedures you are required to follow within your work area.

Dealing with suspicious individuals

Since you are working in the business of hospitality, there will inevitably and frequently be strangers within the building.

As part of your job you should keep yourself alert to the presence of strangers in areas reserved for staff, i.e. in the staff restaurant, offices and corridors. Non-staff may have a legitimate reason for being there: they may be visiting or delivering some material. On the other hand, they may have found their way in and be looking for opportunities to steal.

An individual may seem suspicious to you for a number of reasons. The following list will give you some pointers to potential problems, but remember that behaviour and situations may or may not indicate that an offence is taking place. An individual fitting any of these descriptions might be said to be acting suspiciously:

- someone wearing an incorrect uniform, or a uniform that is ill-fitting or worn incorrectly
- someone asking for directions to certain areas where you would not expect them to work; for example someone wearing kitchen whites and asking directions to a bedroom
- someone carrying company property in an area not open to them
- someone who appears lost or disorientated (remember that they *may* be innocent new employees)
- someone who just *looks* suspicious: perhaps they are wearing heavy clothing in summer, or carrying a large bag into the restaurant. Large bags or coats can be used to remove items from your premises
- someone who seems nervous, startled or worried, or is perspiring heavily
- someone booking into a hotel for a stay without luggage
- a guest asking for details of someone else staying in the establishment. (In this case, it is better to pass on the enquiry rather than give out information to a stranger.)

Responding to a suspicious individual

If you see someone on the premises you do not recognise, or who looks out of place it is important that you:

1 challenge them politely: ask if you can help them, or direct them to the way out
2 report the presence of a stranger to your supervisor immediately.

Procedures for dealing with strangers will vary depending upon the establishment in which you work.

In all cases, *do not put yourself at risk*. Do not approach the person if you feel uncomfortable or potentially threatened by them. Merely reporting any suspicions you have, whether it be about customers, staff or visitors can often be of great help to the security and long term health of the business.

To do

- Find out what procedures are laid down by your organisation for dealing with people acting in a suspicious manner.
- Discuss with your supervisor how you think you might challenge someone should you need to.

Securing storage areas

Throughout the building there will be areas designated as storage, whether for customers or staff. These areas can often be used by a variety of people in the course of a day, so security of the area and the contents are essential.

Storage areas, particularly those allocated for use by customers (such as secure lockers in hotels) are especially sensitive and can lead to a great deal of damage to the business if items from such areas are lost or go missing. Store rooms, refrigerators, freezers and cellars often contain a great deal of stock which constitutes some of the assets of the business; these areas must be protected from potential loss.

Some items can be easily removed from the premises and are therefore of particular concern.

- *Small items* such as linen, cutlery, crockery, food, wine, toiletries, etc. can be easily concealed in a carrier bag or suitcase and removed without too much difficulty.
- *Larger items* such as televisions, irons, hairdryers and computers can also be removed, but will generally need more thought and planning beforehand.
- *Valuables* such as jewellery, watches and money can be easily concealed and removed from the premises and are often more difficult to trace.

It is sometimes extremely difficult to make an area completely secure, especially as the premises are often host to a large variety of people. It is therefore important to minimise the risk as much as possible by following some fundamental guidelines.

Before we explore those guidelines, complete the exercise below. This will help you to identify areas which are not as secure as they could be. This may be due to a lost key, poor working practice or laziness on the part of the staff concerned.

To do

- Draw up a list of all of the designated storage areas within your department and indicate whether they are secured storage areas (i.e. lockable) or unsecured storage areas. Make sure you include every area in your list, including those made available for customers, staff and the storage of company property.
- Once you have drawn up the list, tick those areas which are kept secure at all times. Identify the gaps, then discuss with your colleagues ways of improving the security of these areas.

Securing access

By carrying out regular checks like those given in the example above, you could highlight the need for improvement and increase the security of your area.

The following points show how you might prevent unauthorised access to certain areas.

- Ensure access to storage areas is restricted to specific individuals. This will make it easier to trace any missing items and is likely to reduce the risks.
- Limit the number of duplicate and master keys and keep a record of all key holders. Limiting access to keys makes it easier to control the movement of items around the building.
- Never leave keys lying around or in locks: this is an open invitation to an opportunist thief.
- Never lend keys to other staff, contractors or visitors; especially master keys. If you have been issued with a master key, you have responsibility for the access to that particular storage area.
- Follow any organisational procedures regarding the reporting of lost keys. It may be necessary to trace the lost key or have a new lock fitted to ensure the security of the area.
- If you are working in a hotel, keep guest keys out of sight and reach. If they are visible, it is possible for someone to work out which guests are in or out; if they are within reach, an unauthorised person may take them.
- If you are working in a secure area, e.g. a guest room or liquor store room, always lock the room when you are leaving, even if only for a few moments.

These guidelines are by no means exhaustive, but should help you maintain the security within your area of work and raise your awareness about the potential risks.

To do

- Add your own ideas to the guidelines listed above, taking into account the list of storage areas you drew up earlier.
- Keep the list in a prominent position, such as your notice board or locker to remind you about the 'do's and don'ts' of effective security practice.

Dealing with lost or missing property

From time to time company, customer or staff property may go missing. This can be due to a variety of reasons, such as:
- customer property may have been left behind in a guest room or public area
- company property may have been moved without people knowing and may, in fact, be misplaced rather than lost
- a member of staff may have been careless about returning property, such as dirty linen to the linen room, or crockery to the crockery store
- items may have been stolen from the property. You may hear this type of loss called *shrinkage* or *pilfering*, especially when referring to food or liquor missing from refrigerators or cellars.

In most establishments there will be procedures for dealing with any missing property. If you discover that property has gone missing it is important you follow the correct procedure. The type of information you should report will probably include:
- a description of the missing item/s
- the date and time you discovered the item/s were missing
- the location where item/s are normally stored
- details of any searches or actions taken to locate the item/s.

In some cases your organisation may decide to report the loss to the police. This is common where the item missing is of value or where a substantial amount of goods has gone missing. In some organisations all losses are reported to the police whether theft is thought probable or not. If the police are involved, you may be required to give them information, so it is essential for you to be clear on the circumstances of the losses.

Essential knowledge

Keys, property and areas should be secured from unauthorised access at all times in order to:
- prevent theft
- prevent damage to property
- prevent damage to the business from customer loss of confidence.

Recording lost property

In most establishments there are procedures for recording lost property. This usually covers personal property lost by customers, visitors or staff rather than property which may have been deliberately removed from the premises.

If someone reports they have lost an item it is usual for this to be recorded in a Lost Property Book. A page from one of these is shown below.

- The information required should be recorded clearly and accurately. This information can then be used as a reference point for any property found on the premises.
- When recording lost property it is particularly important to take a contact address or telephone number so that the person can be contacted should the item/s be found.
- If you should find property it is your responsibility to report the find so that it can be returned to the appropriate person.
- In some organisations, found property is retained for a period of, for example, three months and then either returned to the person who reported it or sent to a charity shop.

LOST PROPERTY RECORD

Date/time loss reported	Description of item lost	Where item lost	Lost by (name, address, tel. no.)	Item found (where, when, by whom)	Action taken

A page from a Lost Property Book

What have you learned?

1 Why is it essential to maintain secure storage areas within your establishment?

2 List five potential security risks within your own area.

3 How can you prevent keys from being misused?

4 What should you ensure you do when leaving a secure area?

5 What should you do if you see someone acting in a suspicious manner?

6 How can you reduce the risk of items being taken from your own work area?

Extend your knowledge

1. Find out about the *recovery position* in first aid. When would you need to use this? Why is it effective?
2. Find out what immediate response you could give in the case of: burns and scalds, fainting, strokes and heart attacks.
3. Talk to your security officers. Find out what kind of events they commonly deal with in your establishment.
4. Invite a fire prevention officer to your establishment to talk about fire prevention and fire fighting in more detail.

UNIT G2

Maintaining a professional and hygienic appearance

ELEMENT 1: Maintaining a professional and hygienic appearance

What do you have to do?

- Maintain personal cleanliness and hygiene to the required standards.
- Keep all appropriate clothing, headwear and footwear clean and in good repair.
- Report illnesses and infections in accordance with laid down procedures.
- Comply with all laid down procedures concerning the wear of perfume, cosmetics and jewellery.
- Keep hair, moustaches and beards neat and tidy.
- Treat cuts, grazes and wounds in accordance with laid down procedures.

What do you need to know?

- Why it is important to wear appropriate clothing and footwear.
- The ground rules for good personal hygiene.
- How to deal with wounds and cuts when you are at work.
- Why it is essential to report illness and infection and the procedure you need to follow.

Introduction

The image you project while dealing with customers can say a great deal about the way your company operates. People are more likely to use a restaurant or food outlet if they can see that the staff take care of their appearance and follow good hygiene practices when dealing with food.

As well as looking good, everyone involved in the preparation and service of food has a duty under the Food Hygiene Regulations to protect food from risk of contamination by careful storage and handling. You will find this covered in more detail in Units 2D11 and 2D12 (pages 53 and 99). In food areas in particular there are legal requirements which influence all aspects of the way we work.

As a food handler, you need to be aware of the ways in which your clothes, habits and attention to personal cleanliness can increase or reduce the risk of food contamination. The number of reported cases of food poisoning has been increasing in recent years and many of the outbreaks can be traced back to contamination passing from people to food.

Sources of food poisoning

If you are involved in food handling it is important to be aware of the most common sources of infection so that you can take practical measures to prevent poisoning outbreaks.

There are three main sources of food poisoning:

1 *natural sources,* such as poisonous plants (e.g. toadstools, deadly nightshade). People who eat these plants are likely to develop food poisoning because of the natural poison contained in the plants
2 *chemical or metal contamination,* such as pesticides, cleaning fluids, mercury, lead or copper. Food poisoning from this source can be caused through the chemical being inadvertently spilt into the food
3 *bacteria and germs,* such as salmonella, staphylococcus, clostridium perfringens. These are naturally present all around us and can easily contaminate food if we do not follow good personal hygiene practices. Bacteria are microscopic and invisible to the naked eye, so it is difficult to know when you may be carrying bacteria which can cause food poisoning.
   Bacteria such as staphylococcus is naturally found on the human body, particularly in the ears, nose, throat and on the hands. Other bacteria can be carried in the intestines and can contaminate food through poor personal hygiene, e.g. forgetting to wash hands after using the toilet. Some bacteria, such as salmonella, can be transferred from one source to another through clothes, dirty hands and knives.

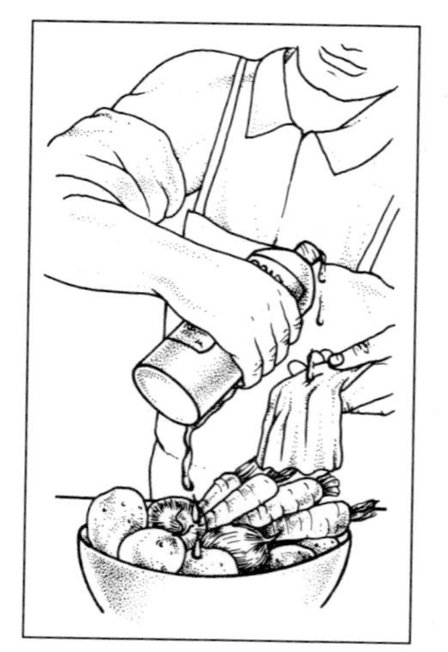

Chemical contamination can occur through accidents in the kitchen

Food Hygiene Regulations

The Food Hygiene Regulations, particularly those related to food handlers, identify and lay down the legal requirements for the main risk areas. We will be covering these more fully later in this chapter (pages 35–8).

Much of the guidance given to food handlers is aimed at reducing the risk of bacterial food poisoning. This is achieved by:

1 protecting the food from contamination through people, by the wearing of protective clothing
2 ensuring that everyone is aware of the main sources of bacteria, i.e. the throat, hair, bowels and hands
3 ensuring that everyone follows basic guidelines on personal hygiene.

Food handler's responsibilities

Under the Food Hygiene (General) Regulations 1970 the food handler's responsibilities are clearly stated.

Food handlers must:
1 protect food from risk of infection
2 wear suitable protective clothing
3 wash hands after visiting the toilet
4 not smoke, spit or take snuff in food rooms
5 cover cuts or wounds with clean washable dressing
6 report illness or contact with illness.

Personal hygiene

In order to reduce the risk of infecting or cross-contaminating food, it is essential for food handlers to observe basic principles of personal hygiene. Most of these principles are common sense and have a place in our daily life, but they need to be emphasised to ensure we comply with our responsibilities under the Food Hygiene Regulations and minimise the risks to ourselves and others.

All of the points listed below are essential parts of good hygiene practice.

Washing your hands regularly prevents germs from contaminating food

Keep your hands clean

Wash hands as often as necessary, but particularly:
- before starting work
- before handling food
- when moving between jobs
- after visiting the toilet
- after touching your nose, hair or ears
- after smoking.

Bacteria on the hands can be one of the main methods of transmitting bacteria and spreading the infection. It may be that you have visited the toilet and have germs on your hand which can easily be spread if you were to return straight to work without washing them.

Finishing one job, such as boning chicken, and then moving on to, for example, mixing mayonnaise may also result in you transferring salmonella bacteria from the chicken to the mayonnaise.

Use disposable tissues in food areas

Germs are present in our ear, nose and throat. It is very easy to transfer bacteria by sneezing without using a tissue, or by spitting or picking our ears or noses, and you should *never* do this. If you need to use a tissue, use a disposable one and wash your hands immediately afterwards.

Keep fingernails short, free from nail polish and use a nail brush to clean them
Bacteria can gather under nails and spread when your hands touch food. It is a legal requirement that all wash hand basins in food preparation areas are equipped with soap, nailbrushes and disposable paper towels or blow dryers.

This water flow for this wash basin is controlled by a knee-operated facility, preventing the hand contact which can cause cross-contamination.

Avoid wearing nail polish, even if uncoloured, as it can chip and fall into food, contaminating it.

Wear only plain rings
Ornate jewellery can harbour bacteria and cause infection. Food particles may also damage the stones, or cause them to fall out. Rings can also be a safety hazard as they can become hot and burn you, or become trapped in machinery.

Keep hair away from food
Food becomes very unappetising if a stray hair has been allowed to fall into it. Hair will carry germs and can infect the food.

The Food Hygiene Regulations require you to:

- wear head covering to reduce the risk of loose hairs falling into food
- keep hair clean by regular washing. This will reduce the risk of bacteria accumulating on hair and may improve general appearance
- keep hair, moustaches and beards neat and tidy. This will reduce risks from bacteria carried on hair
- never comb hair anywhere near food.

General health and personal hygiene

Food handlers should be in good general health. The guidelines given on the next page will help to ensure this.

Staff Sickness Notice

If you develop any illness involving vomiting or diarrhoea, or have come into contact with anyone with these symptoms, you must report it to your Department Manager before commencing work.

Other illnesses you must report to your Manager include: abdominal pain, skin rashes, fever, septic skin, lesions or discharges from your ear, nose or throat.

The Food Hygiene Act requires you to report any sickness

1. Do not work if you have any symptoms linked to food poisoning or have been in contact with someone who has, for example: vomiting, diarrhoea, stomach pains and infections. Report your symptoms to your supervisor. Your kitchen will display a staff notice reminding you to do this.
2. Wash and shower daily to reduce body odour and risks from bacteria. Wear deodorant to reduce the possibility of offensive odours.
3. Cover any cuts or bruises with a clean waterproof dressing. The dressing should be coloured blue so that it can not be 'lost' in food.
4. Avoid working with food if you have any infected and/or unsightly wounds which are likely to cause danger to customers.
5. Avoid bad habits such as:
   - licking fingers when opening bags or picking up paper
   - picking, scratching or touching your nose
   - scratching your head or spots
   - tasting food with an unwashed spoon
   - dipping your fingers into food
   - coughing or sneezing over food
   - smoking
   - using wash hand basins for washing food or utensils.

All of these habits can cause bacteria to spread and *must be avoided at all times.* These habits are also unpleasant to watch and may be off-putting to your customers and colleagues.

Essential knowledge

Illness and infections should always be reported immediately, in order to:
- avoid spreading the disease to other staff
- avoid contamination of food
- allow action to be taken in alerting appropriate people.

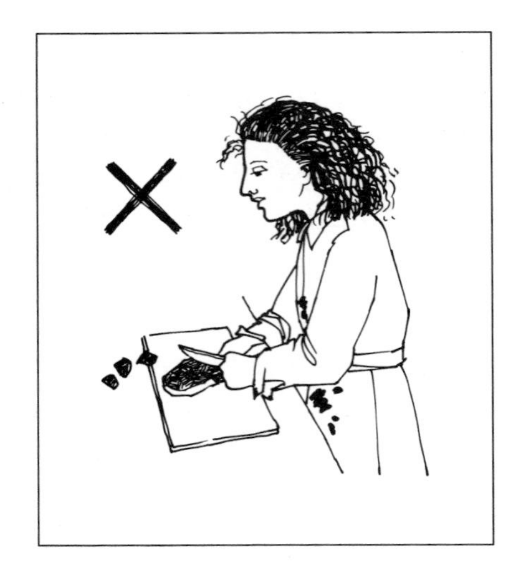

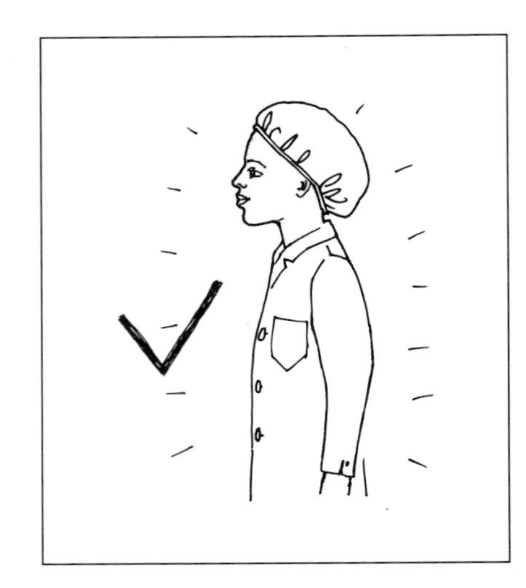

Wear clean, protective clothing

Protective clothing

Protective clothing is specified and required to be worn under the Food Hygiene Regulations. Many companies provide clothing for their staff and it is often the employees' responsibility to ensure they wear the correct clothing and keep it clean and in good repair.

The following guidelines are essential basic practices:

- *wear protective clothing* when in a food preparation area. This helps prevent the risk of transmitting bacteria from your non-work clothing to food. Everyday clothing can easily be contaminated by contact with pets, soil and other people
- *do not wear protective clothing outside food areas,* e.g. to travel to and from work, as this can eliminate its effectiveness
- *keep your protective clothing in good condition,* without tears or missing buttons. Damaged protective clothing can look unsightly and become dangerous if you catch it on machinery, pan handles, edges of worktops, etc.
- *keep your clothing clean and change it daily.* The clothing should be light coloured and washable as food stains and dirt harbour bacteria. Avoid using aprons and kitchen cloths for hand drying as this can lead to cross-contamination
- *keep outdoor footwear separate* from indoor to reduce risks of infection. Alternate the shoes you wear, both to ensure foot odour is kept to a minimum and to protect your feet
- *do not wear worn or open shoes,* as these will not give you adequate protection if a spillage occurs or an article (such as a knife) is dropped onto your feet. Open shoes also offer little support if you happen to slip on a wet floor. Low-heeled, closed shoes give you the most protection and help you move quickly and efficiently about your place of work
- wear clean socks, flesh-coloured stockings or tights to maintain a professional and hygienic appearance.

General appearance

- Avoid wearing too much make-up or perfume as it may seem unpleasant to guests. Strong perfume or aftershave can be transferred to glasses and crockery tainting the food or drink.
- Do not carry excess items in your pockets, such as pens, tissues or money as this can look untidy and unprofessional.

Essential knowledge

Correct clothing, footwear and headgear should be worn at all times in order to:
- maintain a clean and professional appearance
- avoid the risk of contamination of food from hair and bacteria
- ensure personal freshness and eliminate the risk of body odour
- prevent accidents, i.e. through clothes or jewellery coming into contact with machinery
- ensure staff comfort during work periods.

Hygiene checklist

Follow a good personal hygiene practice:
- wash your hair and body regularly
- wear clean protective clothing
- wear protective hair covering and keep your hair tidy
- wash hands after visiting the toilet, touching your hair or face, smoking or preparing food
- use clean utensils and equipment at all times
- use only disposable tissues and towels or hand dryers
- report any illness or contact with ill people to your supervisor immediately
- keep all cuts and wounds covered with a clean waterproof dressing.

To do

- Examine the uniform or protective clothing you wear and check it is clean and in good repair.
- Check yourself against the points listed above to see if you comply with personal hygiene requirements.
- Check that *Wash hands* notices are prominently displayed in wash areas, near wash hand basins and in toilet areas.
- Carry out spot checks to ensure that the wash basins are being used for handwashing only and are supplied with soap, towels and a nail brush.

What have you learned?

1 What are the main causes of food poisoning?

2 Why is it important to wear the correct clothing, footwear and headgear?

3 Which parts of the body can harbour harmful bacteria?

4 When should you wash your hands?

5 Why should illness and infections always be reported?

6 Which areas of the body need to be protected?

7 Give five examples of good personal hygiene practice.

Extend your knowledge

1. Find out which foods are most at risk from bacteria.
2. Carry out some research into the different types of bacteria which can cause food poisoning.
3. Talk to your Local Environmental Health Officer to find out about food poisoning statistics and the most common cause of the problem.
4. Find out more about how the Food Hygiene Regulations relate specifically to food handlers.

UNIT 2D10

Handling and maintaining knives

ELEMENT 1: Handling and maintaining knives

What do you have to do?

- Clean and sharpen knives for use and clean after use according to laid down procedures and satisfying food hygiene regulations.
- Handle and store knives in accordance with laid down procedures.
- Show mastery of basic knife skills.

What do you need to know?

- Why knives should be kept sharp.
- Why knives should be handled correctly.
- The correct use for each knife.
- How to hold and handle your knives correctly and efficiently.
- The main contamination threats when using knives.
- Why it is important to keep preparation and production areas and equipment clean and hygienic.

Introduction

It is very important that you learn to handle, maintain and care for your knives from the beginning of your training as a chef. Given time and practice they will become an extension of your hands.

You will also need to learn how to select the correct knife for the job in hand, such as a filleting knife for filleting fish. During your training you may well come across a great number of cutting, shredding and chopping machines, but none of these can produce the same fine quality of work you will be able to achieve with a sharp knife.

Acquiring these skills takes time and practice. There are certain rules you need to learn before starting to work with knives:

1. always use the knife best suited to the job
2. maintain your knives in a clean and sharp condition
3. handle all knives safely and in a methodical manner

4 once you have chosen the knives you are going to use, place them flat on the work surface with the blade facing inwards
5 never try to catch a knife if it is falling to the floor
6 never leave knives in a sink
7 only ever have one knife on the chopping board at any one time
8 never leave knives on the edge of the table or board
9 never allow knives to become hidden under food items.

Why are these rules important?

Some of these rules will have struck you as common sense, but all of them are commonly broken during training.

1 Choose the correct knife

Failure to do this can be dangerous for a number of reasons, but two of the main ones are as follows:

- if the knife is too large you will not have adequate control over it and you are therefore more likely to have an accident
- if you chose a knife with a rigid blade when you need a flexible blade you will not be able to work as quickly or as efficiently as possible, and you may even have an accident.

2 Keep knives clean and sharp

You must always keep your knives *clean* because:

- you have less control over a dirty, greasy or wet knife
- cutting raw and cooked produce with the same unwashed knife can cause cross-contamination. Always work hygienically.

You must always keep knives *sharp* because:

- a blunt knife requires more pressure to allow it to cut through a food item; this extra pressure can cause loss of control and therefore accidents
- a blunt knife will take longer than a sharp knife to complete a task and the finished result will not be as neat and accurate as when done with a sharp knife.

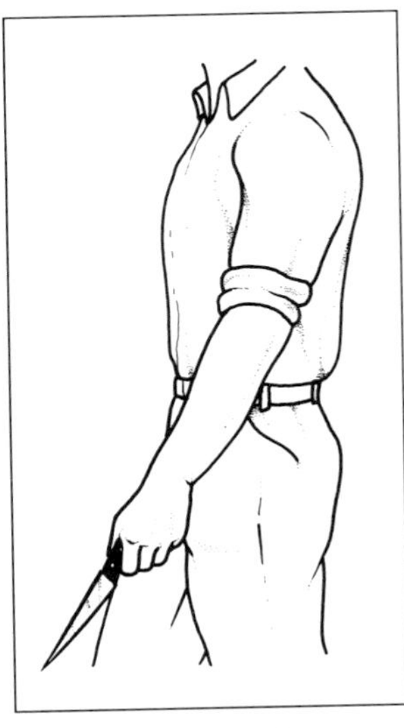

The correct way to carry a knife

3 Handle knives safely and methodically

Careless handling of knives causes accidents.

- Carry knives carefully, by holding the handle, pointing the knife downwards towards the floor with the sharp edge pointing behind you. Keep it slightly away from the body.
- Never transport knives around the kitchen by placing them on a board and then carrying the board. They could easily fall off and cause an accident.
- Never threaten any one with a chef's knife (even in jest) however small its blade may be.

4 Place knives on the workbench carefully

Always place knives flat on the worksurface to avoid the following situations:

- if you allow a knife to stand on the board or work surface with the sharp side of the blade standing upwards someone may

accidently lean on it and cut themselves
- if the blade is left facing outwards from the board and you (or a colleague) then wipe the work area, you may cut yourself.

5 Never try to catch a falling knife
You must never try to save a falling knife, as it is very easy to mistime your catch, so that the blade runs through the palm of your hand. If you drop a knife, allow it to fall, keeping all of your limbs beyond reach.

6 Never leave knives in a sink
Leaving a knife in a sink is often considered to be one of the worst crimes you can commit when learning to handle knives, as it generally results in an accident to someone else rather than to you. Remember that knives in dirty water or full sinks are very difficult to spot.

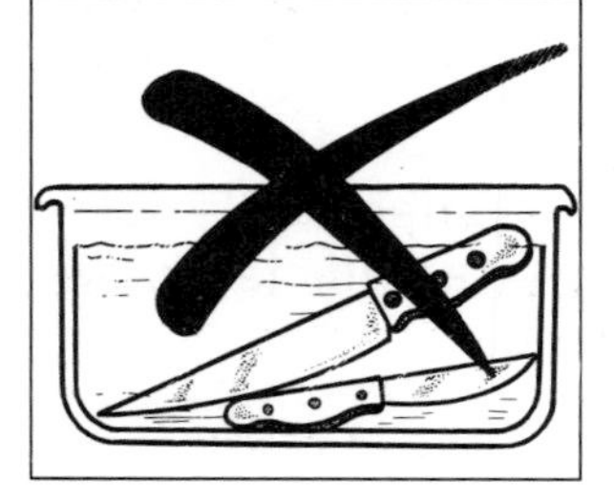

Never leave knives in a sink

7 Never place more than one knife on the chopping board
If you leave any knives other than the one you are using on the chopping board you could catch the other knife with the one you are using; this could result in damage to both knives or an injury to yourself.

8 Place knives on tables with care
You should always keep knives away from the edge of the table as they can easily be knocked off or catch someone walking by who is unable to see them.

9 Keep knives obvious
Do not allow knives to become hidden under food items as there is the same risk of accidental cuts as for *Leaving knives in a sink* (Point 6 above).

Essential knowledge

Knives should always be kept sharp in order to:
- maintain efficiency within food preparation
- keep pressure to a minimum when cutting
- complete tasks more quickly
- avoid risk of accident.

Range of knives

Each knife is produced to perform a particular function. The list given over the next two pages illustrates the types of knives and equipment you should be familiar with, together with the uses of each.

Steel
This is used to sharpen knives. A good steel should have a safety guard.

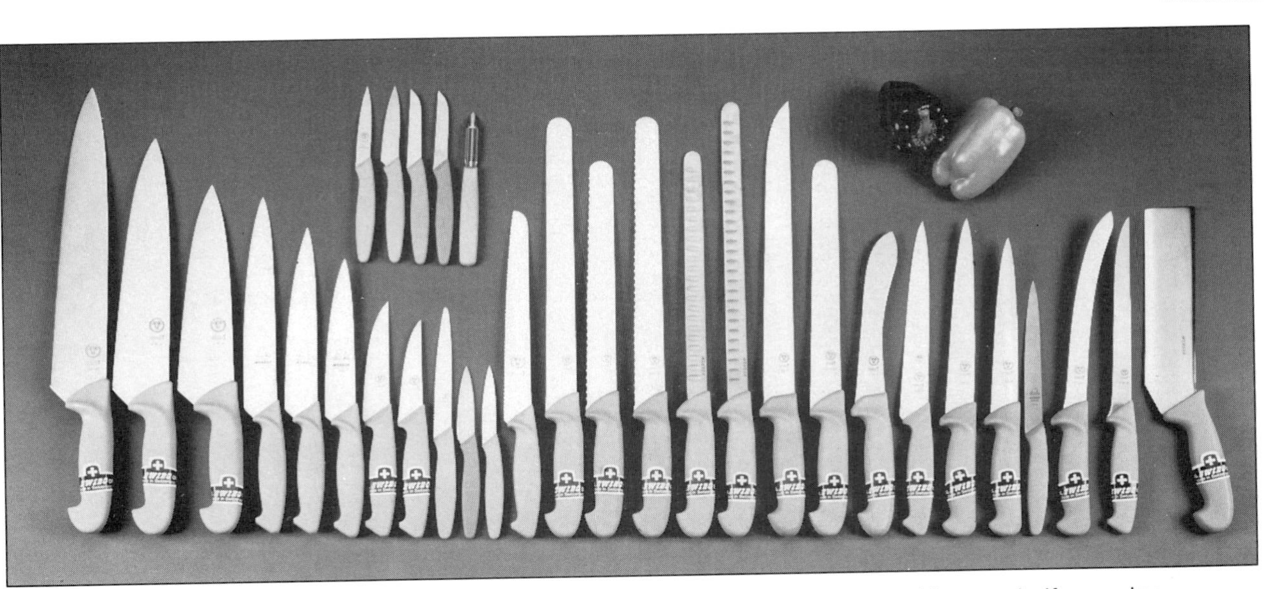

From top left: serrated parer; broad serrated parer; vegetable prep knife; vegetable prep knife; peeler
From bottom left: cook's knife (heavy 12" blade); cook's knife (heavy 10" blade); cook's knife (heavy $8\frac{1}{2}$" blade); cook's knife (light $8\frac{1}{2}$" blade); cook's knife (light $7\frac{1}{2}$" blade); cook's knife (light $6\frac{1}{2}$" blade); vegetable knife (heavy duty 5" blade); vegetable knife (heavy duty 4" blade); multi-purpose knife; broad parer, parer; bread knife; roast beef slicer; 10" slicer; 12" slicer; 10" salmon slicer; 12" salmon slicer; slicer with semi-flexible blade; roast beef slicer; fillet knife with curled rigid blade; meat fillet knife; 8" fillet knife; 7" fillet knife; 6" fish fillet knife; 8" fish fillet knife (curved blade); 8" fish fillet knife (narrow blade); lambnicker

Paring knife
This is a small knife with a thin, slightly flexible blade. It is used for all small hand-held work, such as shaping vegetables.

Cook's knives
The blades of these knives range in size from 10–30 cm (4–12 in). All cook's knives have a rigid blade and are used for a wide range of jobs including shredding, dicing and chopping. They are always used for trimming vegetables, meat, poultry or game. The larger cook's knives can be used to chop through young porous bones of meat or poultry.

Filleting knives
The blades of these can range from 15–20 cm (6–8 in) or even longer. They have a very thin and flexible blade and are used to fillet fish.

Boning knives
The blade size of these ranges from 13–17 cm (5–$6\frac{1}{2}$ in). The blade can be straight or curved to suit large and small butchery. The blades are generally rigid but it is possible to buy boning knives with a slightly flexible blade. They are used to remove bones from joints of meat.

Steak knives
These range in size from 20–30 cm (8–12 in). A steak knife has a curved end and is specially designed to cut through raw meat, e.g. sirloin and rump steaks.

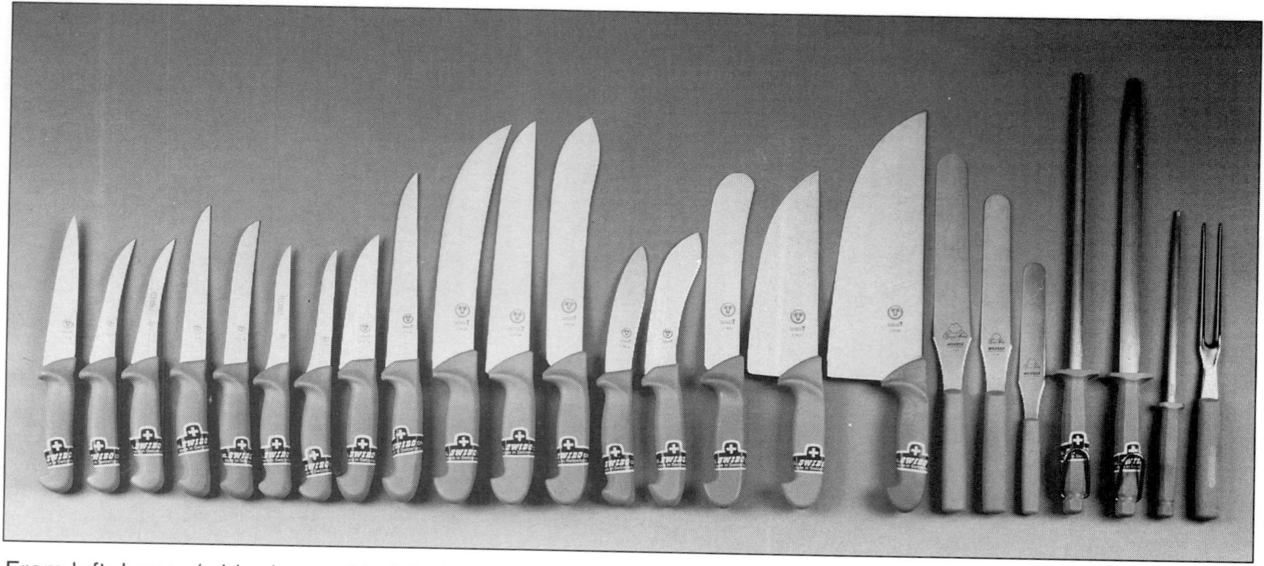

From left: boner (wide dagger blade); American boner (rigid blade); American boner (flexible); boner (rigid); Scandinavian boner; boner (flexible blade); boner (rigid); European boner; boner (long rigid blade); scimitar; European butcher's knife; Butcher's knife; sheep skinning knife; dough knife; Italian butcher's knife; heavy Italian butcher's knife; spatula; spatula; spatula; steel (round blade) steel (oval blade); household steel; fork

Slicers

These knives come in many different forms and are sometimes called by another name by manufacturers: you may see them called *meat knives* or *carvers*. The blades may have serrated or plain edges, and can be anything from 25–36 cm (10–14 in) long. Some have pointed ends while others have rounded ends. They are used to slice cooked meats, smoked salmon and even bread.

Deep-freeze knives

These knives are specially designed with a serrated blade to saw through frozen meat or fish. This type of knife is very specialised and is not part of every knife set.

Palette knives

These vary in length and width; some are plain edged while others have serrated edges. The blade is always flexible and rounded at the top. They are used for:

- moulding and shaping items, such as puréed potato
- turning items over whilst cooking, such as shallow-fried fish
- applying icing/cream to pastries and gateux
- carving (serrated-edge palette knives only).

Oyster knife

This is a special knife used to prize open oyster shells. It has a rigid blade with a rounded point and a guard at the end of the handle.

Fork

A fork used by a chef has long and very sharp prongs. It is used to lift meat and poultry out of trays without piercing the flesh (which would allow the natural juices to escape).

Zesters
These are used to remove the thin layer of the outer skin from citrus fruits.

Vegetable peelers
These are used to peel all types of vegetables. They have a sharp point at the end which is used to remove eyes and blemishes from vegetables.

Apple corers
These are used to remove the core from apples, pears, etc.

Poultry secateurs
These are used for cutting through poultry bones. Most have serrated blades and are spring loaded to make cutting easier.

Fish scissors
These are used to cut away fins and trim tails on all types of fish.

Holding a knife

When practising your knife skills it is important to learn how to hold a knife in the correct manner.

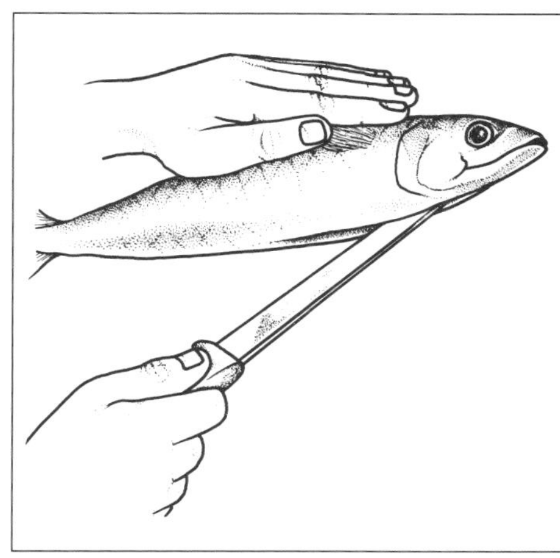

Left: the correct way to hold a boning knife
Right: the correct way to hold a filleting knife

If you were to hold a cook's knife in the same way that you hold a knife when eating you would have your hand around the handle and your first finger pointing down the blade. This is not the way to hold a cook's knife as it would not give you enough control. Instead, place the knife into your hand so that your thumb and first finger are grasping the blade but are not underneath the heel of the knife (or you will cut yourself). This may feel uncomfortable until you get used to it. When holding the knife correctly the blade should not be able to wobble about in your hand.

You would hold a filleting knife in the same way, but you should work with it keeping the blade horizontal (rather than vertical) in your hand most of the time.

The most notable exception to this method is the boning knife, which is generally held like a dagger. Note that the holding method depends on the joint being boned out.

Sharpening knives

The most traditional method of maintaining a sharp edge on a knife is by using a steel. Sharpening a knife can be a dangerous exercise if not done with care.

Read through the following instructions then practise with your knife, referring back to the text when necessary. *Do not try to sharpen a knife whilst reading the text as this could be dangerous.*

1. Select a steel and the knife you wish to sharpen.
2. Hold the steel in one hand with its point away from you and pointing slightly upwards.
3. Holding the knife firmly in the other hand, start by placing the hilt of the blade at the base of the steel.
4. Angle the knife at approximately 18° then firmly draw the blade across the steel.
5. Repeat this process by placing the knife on the underside of the steel.
6. Repeat Steps 4 and 5 several times.
7. To test for sharpness, carefully and gently draw your finger over the blade. It should feel slightly abrasive.
8. Now wash the knife to remove any filings that might be on the blade.

Sharpen your knife each time you come to use it or if it goes dull during use.

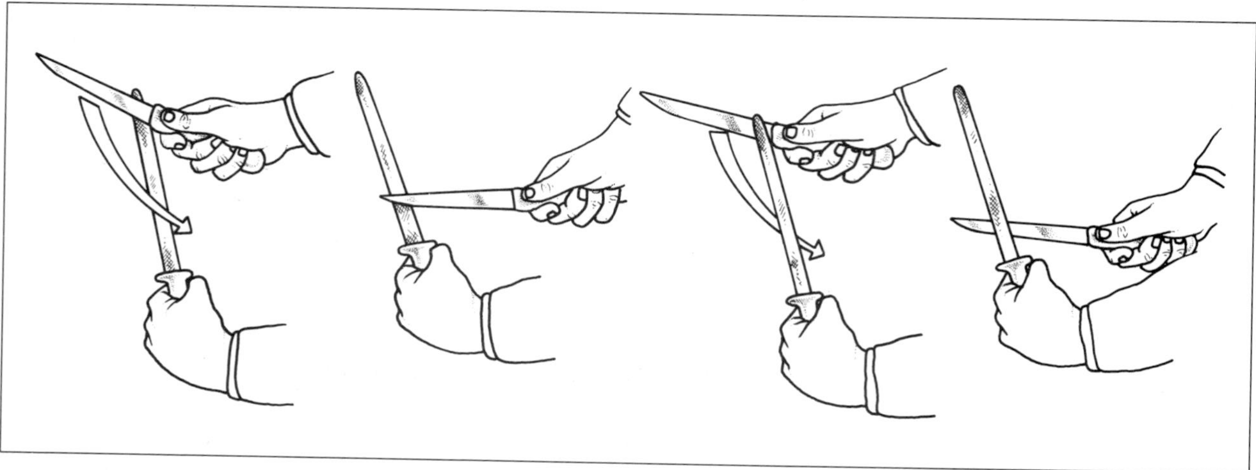

Sharpening a knife

Essential knowledge

Knives should always be handled correctly in order to:
- avoid accidents to people
- avoid accidents to food items
- maintain a safe and secure work area
- obtain the required effect when cutting, chopping and slicing.

Knife safety

Carrying knives

Carrying knives around the kitchen can be very dangerous. They should be carried with the point aimed downwards, held slightly away from the body, and with the sharp edge of the blade facing backwards.

You should *never* carry a knife with the point facing in front of you as someone could easily be hurt. Nor should you carry knives around on chopping boards as they may well slip off while you are carrying the board.

Maintaining knives

Good maintenance of your knives is essential for many reasons, from health and safety aspects to prolonging the life of your equipment. The following points need to be considered when maintaining knives:
- always keep knives clean, as you may be using them on both cooked and raw foods
- make sure the handles of knives are clean: if they are greasy they could cause the knife to slip during use
- always wash knives in hot water with detergent and then rinse them well
- when drying your knives, always make sure that the sharp side of the blade is facing away from you and that your fingers are not over the cutting edge
- store the clean knives safely by placing them back into their carrying wallet or a case specially adapted to hold them in individual compartments.

Knives in a carrying case

Never just throw your knives into a box, drawer or locker. They should always be placed into some form of compartmental holder to prevent you having an accident while searching for a particular knife. Searching through a pile of knives for the one that you want is also time wasting.

Health, safety and hygiene

Make sure that you are familiar with the general points given in Units G1 and G2 (pages 1–41). Pay special attention to the sections on cross-contamination from raw and cooked foods using cutting implements (both mechanical and hand-held).

Cross-contamination is the transfer of harmful bacteria from one contaminated surface to another. The knife is an ideal vehicle in the transfer train due to its versatility. It is therefore essential for health, hygiene and safety reasons to methodically wash and clean each knife after use and immediately before starting a new task. Particular attention must be paid to cleanliness when using knives to work on first raw, then cooked foods, or from one type of food item to another.

Remember that the surface of the knife may appear clean to the naked eye but may actually be holding bacteria (evident under a microscope). This bacteria will be transferred to the next surface you cut. Always use a bactericidal detergent or sanitiser when cleaning knives and use a fresh disposable wipe to dry them. Dispose of the wipe immediately after use.

The risks of cross-contamination will only be minimised by constant vigilance in your approach.

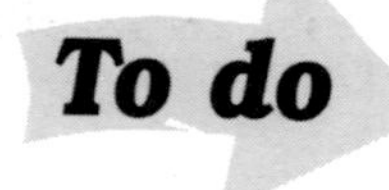

- Find an example of each of the knives and cutting implements listed on pages 44–7.
- Watch your chef using a boning knife. Notice how they hold the knife and what safety precautions they take.
- List the reasons why you must always keep your knives sharp.
- Watch your supervisor chopping vegetables. Which knife do they use? What techniques do they use?
- Watch your supervisor cleaning a knife after use. What chemicals and materials do they use?

Unexpected situations

If someone is cut by a knife, first establish the severity of the cut.

For a minor wound:

1. clean the wound (under running water or with a swab) then dry it gently
2. press a swab or dressing against the wound and raise the injured part to slow the flow of blood (where possible)
3. look after the injured person, keeping them calm, warm and as comfortable as possible
4. contact your first aider.

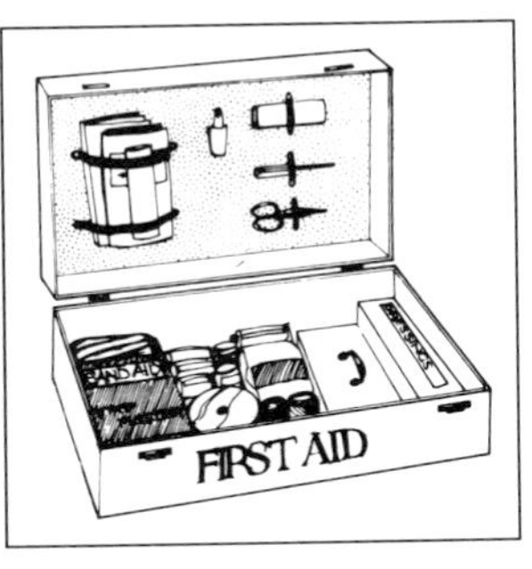

First aid kit

For a major wound:

1 *place a dressing over the wound* (large enough to cover the area easily)
2 *bandage over the dressing,* tying it firmly enough to control the bleeding but not so tightly that it affects circulation
3 *call for urgent medical help.* This might include calling both your own first aider and an ambulance.

Remember:

- a wound more than 1.75 cm (1/2 in) in length may need stitching in hospital
- blood can carry the HIV virus (which causes AIDS). Cover any cuts or grazes on your own hands with a waterproof dressing before attending to a wound, and always wash your own hands before and after treating wounds.

What have you learned?

1 Why should knives always be kept sharp?

2 Why should you keep knives in a compartmentalised holder?

3 What would you use the following implements for:

- a filleting knife?
- a cook's knife?
- a steak knife?

4 Why should you always handle knives correctly?

____

____

____

5 Why should knives always be kept clean?

____

____

____

Extend your knowledge

1. Contact a knife supplier for further information, such as: Andrew Nisbet and Co Ltd, Unit 1, Waterloo Street, Old Market, Bristol BS2 0PH.
2. Compare different sets of knives. Look at how they are made and compare their weights. Heavier knives often indicate quality.
3. If you are considering buying a knife, test several before making a choice. Is the handle, size and weight suited to you?
4. Watch other people using knives that you would not normally use. Notice the different holding techniques and methods used.

Accepting and storing food deliveries

ELEMENTS 1 AND 2: Accepting food deliveries and maintaining food stores

What do you have to do?

- Tally the food deliveries by comparing the order sheet and delivery note, checking visually.
- Check food deliveries for damage and to ensure that the *best before* date is acceptable
- Monitor the temperature of deliveries in line with food hygiene legislation.
- Transfer food delivery items to their storage areas without damaging them.
- Store delivery items under the correct conditions according to laid down procedures.
- Complete delivery documentation correctly.
- Keep accurate records of received, stored and issued food items.
- Report any low food stock levels to the appropriate person.
- Handle all food items with care to preserve their quality during storage, issue and return.
- Keep receiving and storage areas clean and tidy.
- Prevent unauthorised access to receiving and storage areas.
- Work in an organised and efficient manner according to laid down procedures.

What do you need to know?

- How to store food correctly to prevent damage during storage.
- Why food must be used by its *best before* date.
- What the correct stock rotation procedures are for each food type.
- Why a constant stock of food items should be maintained.
- Why deliveries must tally with both the order and delivery documentation.
- Why receiving and storage areas must be secured from unauthorised access at all times.
- Why correct storage and rotation procedures should be followed.
- How to deal with unexpected situations.
- How to plan your work taking account of priorities and daily schedules.

Introduction

The store function of any food operation is the nerve centre of the business. Every caterer must know how to purchase foods, check that the correct quality and quantity of foods are delivered, ensure the paperwork tallies and that the food is moved into the correct storage conditions until required for preparation and production.

The attention paid to cost, storage and quality of all food items affects the viability of any food operation. The volume of food ordered and stored determines the value of stock held, which in turn affects the cash flow position of the business. This is critical, especially for small businesses.

Stores can be very large facilities designed for every type of food item (such as in a large hotel) or they can consist of a few shelves, a refrigerator, freezer and a dry cupboard (such as in a small restaurant). Whatever the storage facility, it is still important to check all food upon delivery, making sure that it meets your cost, quality and quantity requirements. In this way you can ensure that you are producing the best product at the lowest cost.

The range of food items available today require a wide variety of storage conditions and types. Food may be delivered in various states (raw, chilled, frozen, etc.), all of which need particular storage conditions. Failure to ensure that food is stored at the correct temperature and humidity, that stock is rotated according to date of purchase and that packaging is not damaged in any way can lead to food becoming unfit to eat, spoiled or reduced in its shelf life. Serious problems can occur as a result of inadequate storage, such as mould growth, infestation by insects, rancidity, etc.

Food items start to decompose as soon as they are taken from the sea, ground, or, in the case of meats, when the animal is killed. Storage conditions should reduce the *rate* of decomposition, to preserve the flavour, nutritional value, colour and appearance of foods. During storage food should not be exposed to risk of contamination or damage.

Large dry stores facility

Checking for damage

All deliveries should be checked carefully. Perishable foods should be checked immediately and moved to cold storage, deep freezers or refrigerators without delay. Any damaged or discoloured packaging should be rejected. Leaking cartons or containers, split bags, crushed boxes, broken eggs and bulging tins are not acceptable and should not be accepted into the store. Do not take delivery of any goods that are past their *use by* or *best before* date. It is important that these and any other food item that does not meet with the product specifications as agreed by contract or by order are sent back upon delivery with the items noted.

Recording delivery

The delivery note sent with the food items you have ordered enables you to check that the foods ordered match the food items delivered. It will contain the following information:

- *supplier details;* i.e. name, address, VAT registration number
- *details of your establishment;* i.e. the organisation's name, address, account number, delivery code and invoice number
- *a list of the items ordered,* showing the number of units ordered and quanitity per unit
- *details of 'out of stock' items,* or '*items to follow*'.

Delivery notes usually come in duplicate or triplicate forms. Check through the delivery note, marking a cross against each item that has been delivered. Once the entire delivery has been checked the delivery note is separated into two parts: one part is left with the stores person; the second part (and third if applicable) is returned to the supplier as a record that the items have been delivered, recorded and accepted.

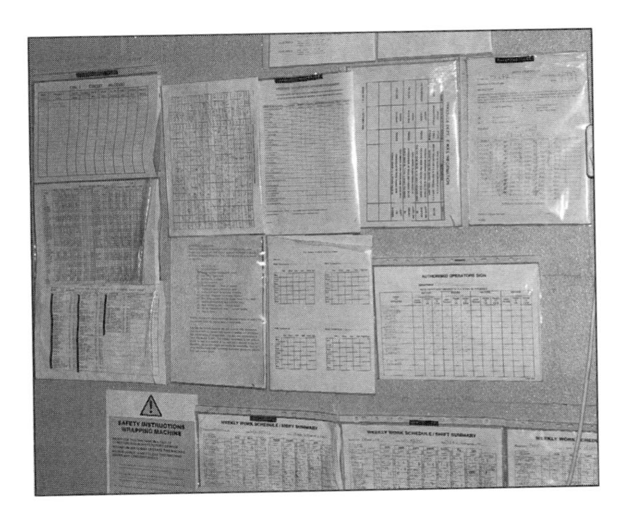

Daily delivery and order sheets

Occasionally your stores may be closed when a delivery is made, as delivery schedules are not always accurate. This means that someone other than the stores person will need to accept deliveries. It is important for you to be aware of recording and checking procedures to ensure that you can deal with this situation should it arise.

Recording returned items

Records of these unacceptable foods need to be checked against weekly and/or monthly invoices to ensure that you are not charged for items returned. The returned items should not appear on the invoice, or if they do, a credit note should be issued against them (see below). As soon as you notice that goods are unacceptable, you must take action immediately by notifying the supplier and recording the returned items. If you delay in notifying the supplier they may not accept responsibility.

Invoices

Invoices are bills that itemise foods and products delivered, together with individual and total costs for each product. Items subject to VAT will be listed with the price before VAT, the VAT due, and the total cost. These details enable any VAT returns to be made by your organisation.

Invoices should contain the following information:

- *supplier details;* i.e. name, address, telephone number, telex and/or fax number, VAT registration number
- *details of your establishment;* i.e. the organisation's name, address and account number
- *the heading 'Invoice'*, together with details of the delivery date of the order, the invoice number and details of all products supplied (including prices, separate VAT charges, items that are *to follow* or were *out of stock*)
- *details of terms of settlement* and any discount-related information.

Credit notes

Credit notes are issued where details of goods listed on an invoice were incorrect; this may be because the items were not delivered, or because the cost given on the invoice was incorrect. A credit note will confirm the amount of deduction made against the invoice, and usually lists the items and costs to be credited to the purchaser.

Statements

These provide a summary of a number of invoices and credit notes sent to an organisation over a specific period of time (usually one month). The statement will list any outstanding charges from previous statements together with details of invoices issued in the period since the last statement.

Note that *Interest added* details are sometimes added. These will inform you of any price reductions applicable if you pay within a certain time, and they are included to encourage prompt payment.

Essential knowledge

Deliveries must tally with both the order and delivery documentation in order to:

- check that the food ordered tallies with the foods delivered
- identify shortages of any food item upon delivery and inform both the delivery person and supplier straight away
- ensure that a credit note is issued for any foods not delivered but listed as delivered on the delivery note
- check that the price of food ordered corresponds to the invoiced price. Suppliers often alter prices without notification. The conditions of sale agreed between the supplier and the customer need to be checked. You have the right to return goods where a notification clause does not exist but prices are higher than those agreed when the food is ordered
- eliminate pilfering prior to delivery by careful monitoring of all food deliveries
- maintain stock control procedures.

To do

- Check a delivery of dry stores. Make copies of the order and delivery sheets and make sure that you are familiar with how to complete them.
- Find out whether your establishment keeps a Breakages Book for insurance claims to be made.
- Find out at what point in a delivery the goods should be signed for.

Suppliers and purchasing

In order to know how to check food for quality when accepting deliveries, you will need to know what kind of quality indicators are used when a food buyer is looking to purchase food. When buying raw food materials it is important to buy the best materials at the most effective cost. This does not always mean that you should buy foods because they are cheap; if you buy cheap, poor quality produce this may be reflected in the dishes you produce. Remember that foods purchased in season will always be cheaper than those out of season. Bulk buying is usually cheaper, but only buy in bulk if the storage capacity is available. In the case of meat, only buy in bulk either when it can be used as soon as it has hung for the optimum time, or when it can be frozen below –18 °C (64 °F) and used before freezer burn develops.

Over time you will begin to recognise the normal price ranges and cost fluctuations of different foods. Always buy from reputable traders, dealing with two or three traders offering the same range of foods. This will establish your company as a worthwhile business for the traders involved, and they will work towards keeping you as a customer. If they deliver poor quality, stale/old, unsound or even unripe foods, send them back immediately. Once traders know that you will not accept second-class goods they will quickly learn the standard of quality you expect.

Always ensure that the cost of the food is realistic, and that the delivered foods are of good quality, undamaged, fresh and chilled (where necessary).

Choosing a supplier

When using a supplier for the first time, you might like to work through the following points:

- check that your supplier knows and complies with the hygiene regulations
- find out whether all their staff have (at least) a basic qualification in food hygiene
- draw up detailed product specifications, to ensure the foods you order are the foods you receive
- visit the supplier's premises to check where your supplies come from
- find out which other customers they supply. Phone these establishments to check on the service. Are they satisfied?
- ensure that raw and cooked foods are not delivered in the same containers
- check the condition of the delivery van or lorry. Do the drivers smoke?
- dry foods are often overlooked: check that any packaging is sound and undamaged
- check that chilled foods *are* chilled. You can check by touching them, or, preferably, by using a probe and hygienic wipes to test the delivered temperature. This is important for chilled foods, especially high risk dairy products and high-protein food items.

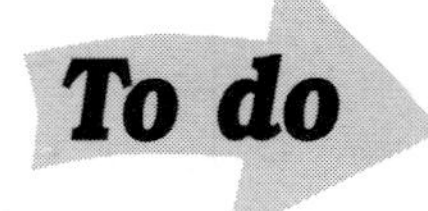

- Find out whether purchasing specifications are provided for your suppliers.
- Find out the unit costs for fresh meat and poultry from three different suppliers.
- Find out whether your establishment buys vegetables that are out of season. Ask whether the price differs when the food is in season and by what amount.

Establishing food quality

Later in this chapter we will list the particular qualities to look for in types of food. However you can assess the general quality of food delivered by smell, taste, appearance and texture.

Smell
Good food should smell fresh. There should be a natural, not unpleasant smell; any odd smell should invite closer inspection. Fish and dairy products need careful inspection where smell is concerned. If whole fish feels dry rather than slimy, your sense of smell will confirm whether it is fresh or not. Sometimes fishmongers may sell defrosted fish as fresh; you need to be able to tell the difference.

Taste
Taste is always an excellent communicator of quality. If you are in doubt about how a particular type of food should taste, check with someone more experienced.

Appearance
When delivered, food should look fresh, clean, undamaged, and visibly free from spoilage, slime, mould or fungal growth. One mouldy tomato or vegetable can and will turn all the stock mouldy within days.

Frozen foods need close inspection. Excess ice on packaging might indicate partial thawing and re-freezing. Check for signs of freezer burn on foods.

Texture
Check whether the food feels firm, soft or hard. Measure this against how it should feel. What is its usual texture?

Accepting deliveries of different food types

Meat and poultry deliveries

Weighing meat items upon delivery

Meat and poultry are the most expensive food items purchased and must always be handled carefully. When meat and poultry are delivered always check for freshness and quality. Make sure that there is no bruising, that the meat is not sticky and does not have an unpleasant smell.

Weigh each item to check that it corresponds to the delivery note and the order sheet, using clean paper on the scale pan each time to prevent contamination. Remember to wipe clean the scales each time, and to wash your hands between handling different meats and poultry.

When best ends of meat are delivered, check how much of the shoulder blade has been left in: it should be no longer than 1–2 cm ($^{1}/_{2}$–1 in). If you are unsure of the specifications, check with the chef or your supervisor. Meat and poultry are very costly; the foods should be good quality, chilled when delivered and packaged separately, not thrown in one box or tray. If you are accepting a delivery including mince, check that it is lean. Do not accept large percentages of fat.

The quality purchasing points for raw meat and poultry are covered in Unit 2D1: *Preparing meat and poultry for cooking* in the Cookery Units book, pages 25–56.

The following points are important when purchasing and accepting deliveries of meat and poultry:
- order the correct quantity
- order the appropriate cut or joint for a particular product
- buy meat or poultry of the best quality according to the price paid and intended purpose
- know that the meat or poultry delivered is sound, fit for its intended purpose and fresh
- check that the meat or poultry is of the weight ordered
- store correctly according to the meat type until required for preparation
- tally the price of the meat and poultry as ordered with the invoice.

Fish deliveries

At one time fish was considered inferior to meat and poultry and prices reflected this. However, as seas have become over-fished and general consumption has risen, the price has also risen and it is no longer seen as a cheap alternative to meat or poultry. The price per kilo is now high, and care when purchasing and storing fish is not just essential but fundamental to effective food operations today.

Fish can be bought and delivered in various forms:
- whole to be skinned, filleted and portioned
- skinned and filleted ready for portioning
- as steaks (darnes) or prepared to your requirements
- pre-frozen, pre-portioned ready to be finished
- frozen, portioned and finished ready to cook.

The fishmonger needs to know exactly how your fish should be prepared. If you are involved in ordering fish, always provide a detailed specification to prevent any misunderstandings.

As fish is now regularly available both fresh and frozen, most operations purchase fish perhaps two to three times per week. Always buy fish as near to the time of use as possible.

Fish needs to be fresh and firm with a clean smell. The general appearance should be clean and bright, and the skin should be covered with a moist transparent outer slime. The gills should be bright and the eyes not sunken.

Check for freshness by pressing against the fish skin with your finger: if an impression remains after you have lifted your finger off the fish is not fresh. Always look inside the belly flaps for signs of fresh blood, and notice whether the flesh is firmly attached to the bones. If whole fish are delivered in a soft condition, this can indicate either that the fish has just finished spawning or that it is not fresh; in either case it will not cook well.

When accepting a delivery of flat fish overfillets, check that you have an equal number of white and dark skin fillets. Some fishmongers will give you up to 70 per cent of dark fillets and only 30 per cent of white.

The quality purchasing points for fresh fish are given in Unit 2D2: *Preparing and cooking fish dishes* of the Cookery Units book.

Key points in accepting fish deliveries

The following points are important when buying or accepting deliveries of fish:

- when accepting delivery of frozen fish check whether it is still frozen or thawing
- when accepting delivery of any fresh fish or shellfish, ensure they are fresh
- make sure that the fish is one that is in season. Be wary of fresh fish available out of season
- weigh all fish and shellfish products upon delivery
- check that live lobsters are alive, blue in colour and moving
- make sure that any shellfish that are live (such as mussels and oysters) are tightly shut; any that are open upon delivery should not be accepted
- when accepting delivery of trout or small whole fish, check that no older stale fish have been mixed in with the fresh ones. On the older fish the skin will be dry and dull with a soft texture
- notice how the fish is packed. Are the fish in separate boxes? Each fish should be boxed individually, to prevent cross-contamination of smell or juices
- always change the wrapping that fish is delivered in and place the fish on a clean plastic or stainless steel tray. If you wash fresh fish it should be used within 12 hours or frozen
- check how many fillets were ordered against how many have been delivered
- keep separate deliveries separate: do not mix yesterday's delivery with today's
- only buy from a reputable trader. Be wary of a 'cheap deal' or someone 'doing you a favour'

- check that you know all the basic cuts of fish, how they are ordered and what they look like. If you have ordered 150 g (5 oz) of fillets, weigh them, multiply this by the number of fillets and check the total weight against the cost per kilo. An unscrupulous fishmonger may try to charge you for more than you have received.

Fruit and vegetable deliveries

Accepting fruit deliveries

Fresh fruit and vegetables can make or break a good meal. They need to be fresh and purchased in season (where possible) to keep cost to a minimum. They must be stored correctly to obtain maximum shelf life and to retain their essential nutrient value and food quality.

Knowing when fruit and vegetables are in season is a good guide for estimating their cost. Vegetables and fruits that are out of season will cost more because they will have been imported. Some specialist types of lettuce and certain fruits are costly even when in season; check that you are familiar with these types. The selling price of the eventual dish will need to reflect the increased food cost when these items are used.

The fresh fruit and vegetable market is one of the most difficult areas in which to buy food. The produce is highly perishable, and if it is too ripe when bought it quickly deteriorates past the point of being edible, unless used immediately. If it is not ripe enough when bought it will not be enjoyable to eat.

A sound knowledge of quality purchase points for fresh vegetables and fruit is essential. When buying or accepting deliveries of fresh vegetables, key points should be used to identify the quality, degree of freshness and ripeness of fruit and vegetables, as given in the following sections.

Key points when accepting vegetable deliveries

It is important when purchasing fruit and vegetables to:

- purchase as near to the time of use as is possible
- check that the quality on delivery is correct
- return any fruit and vegetables not fitting the purpose for which they are intended
- weigh high-cost fruit and vegetable items and tally them with the delivery note
- store the fruit and vegetables correctly to ensure optimum quality and shelf life.

Deliveries of vegetable types

Root vegetables

Root vegetables such as carrots, beetroot, radishes, celeriac, swedes, salsify and parsnips need to be firm, clean, in season, free from bruising or decomposition, and without any visible mould or fungal growth. Root vegetables should be free from soil and undamaged by cuts from cultivation machinery. Fine root shoots are an indication of age. Check that any carrots are not soft or spongy. As the season progresses the root vegetables become larger in size; small (baby) vegetables are available at the start of their season and command high prices.

Potatoes

These need to be fresh and firm with no signs of growing shoots (which is an indication of old age). Check that none of them have signs of decomposition which will quickly spread during storage. On delivery, open potato bags to view the produce you are buying.

Bulbs

- *Chives* should be bright green, fine and without discolouration or decay.
- *Leeks* should be clean, firm and plump. They should not be limp or damaged, or show any sign of yellowness or wilting. If they have been grown in soot or soil trenches they will need to be split and washed very thoroughly before use.
- *Onions, shallots and garlic* should have a dry, crisp, unbroken outer skin and show no signs of sprouting. They should be even in size and firm to the touch. Softness and moisture are signs of decay and age.

Leaf vegetables

- *Cabbage* should be crisp, with no signs of rust or damage to the leaf structure. White cabbage should be heavy and compact with a very close leaf structure. Red cabbage should be reddish-purple, firm and compact. Check for signs of limpness or dehydration.
- *Chard* should be firm and dark green with a white coloured stem. They are best when eaten young, so check that the leaves are not large (an indication of age).

- *Chicory* should be crisp, with a fresh appearance and no traces of browning or blemishes.
- *Endive* should have tightly packed, long, blanched leaves. Check that all the leaves are firm and closed with no sign of browning on the outer edges (this indicates age and decay).
- *Lettuce* should be crisp, with a firm heart and no rotting or decaying leaves. Check for fly infestation and slug or caterpillar damage, and for mechanical damage during storage and transportation. Also check for brown rust disease.
- *Spinach* should have fresh, deep-green leaves with no signs of decay. Small stalks are are indication of youth and quality; larger stalks can be tough.
- *Sprouts* and sprout tops should be small, compact and bright green in colour. Check that the leaves are tightly packed, with no browning on the leaf edge (this indicates a long storage period). If sprouts are delivered in green nets, always open the nets and check the actual leaf condition, as the netting masks the true colour of the sprout.
- *Watercress* should have fresh bright green leaves, and be packed in bunches displaying the grower's label. Check that there is no visible root growth and that the leaves are not yellowing.

Flowers

- *Artichokes (globe)* should have a compact flower head with the leaves packed closely around the head. *Artichoke bottoms* are taken from large artichokes, and form the base of growth for the flower head.
- *Broccoli* should be firm and have a good colour: either green or purple. There should be no sign of discolouration or yellow-brown wilt.
- *Cauliflower* should have a compact, well-formed white head, with a close, tightly packed structure. Look for signs of decay in the head itself, which should be very firm.

Fruit vegetables

- *Aubergines* should be firm and plump, with a waxy, glossy, dark purple skin.
- *Courgettes* should be firm, crisp and not too large. There should not be any sign of softness or skin blemish. Look for signs of decay.
- *Cucumbers* should be firm and crisp. Choose long, straight narrow ones rather than curled, wide fruits. Check for signs of limpness.
- *Marrows* should be firm with a good green colour. Avoid marrow with very tough skins.
- *Peppers* (capsicums) come in green, red, yellow and white/cream colours. They should be crisp and firm with no signs of softness or decay.
- *Tomatoes* should be ripe with a bright red colour and a firm, even shape.

Seed and stem vegetables

- *Asparagus* should have long narrow stems with a tight, closed head. Check for signs of browning or wrinkling at the ends of the stalk which indicates that the asparagus is not fresh.
- *Celery* should be white, firm and very crisp without signs of rust or mechanical damage. Check for insect damage and decay.
- *Fennel* should be firm with a bulbous-shaped swollen base. Check for signs of browning or split damage to the base.
- *Kohlrab*i should be firm and heavy. Choose the young, smaller kohlrabi which are more tender than the larger, older vegetables.
- *Seakale* should be a bright, white colour with a firm, crisp texture. Check for blemish and discolouration.
- *Sweetcorn* is available as small baby corn or as larger cob heads. The corn should be firm and full, not limp or soft.

Legumes

- *Broad beans* should have a firm, broad, green pod. They should not be too limp.
- *French beans* should be crisp, firm, straight and green in colour. Choose the smaller ones where possible.
- *Mangetout* are crisp, flat peas used whole. They should be a bright green colour.
- *Peas* should be crisp and firm with a plump shape. They are usually purchased frozen.
- *Runner beans* are best when young and small with a good green colour. Larger, wilted beans are tough and stringy.

Fungi

- *Ceps (cèpes*) are sometimes called *flat mushrooms*, because they are fleshy, flat and brown. Choose the smaller, young cèpes with no mechanical damage.
- *Morels* (sponge mushrooms) have a conical pitted cap with a brown to yellow colour. They are best young and fresh.
- *Mushrooms* (cultivated as small button, cup or open flat mushrooms) should be firm and white when small, becoming deeper brown in colour as they open to cup and flat forms. They should be unbroken with no damage or blemishes.
- *Truffles* come in white and black forms. The black type has a hard, rough skin with a strong aroma and they should be even in size. The white truffle has a more pronounced flavour, with a strong scent and taste.

From left to right: ceps, morels, button mushrooms, truffles

Fruits

- *Citrus fruits* (e.g. grapefruits, lemons, mandarins, oranges) should have smooth, firm skins and compact fruits.
- *Hard fruits* (e.g. apples, pears) should be crisp and firm with a pleasant aroma. Check for signs of blemish or bruising.
- *Soft fruits* or berries (e.g. blackberries, cranberries, currants, gooseberries, loganberries, raspberries, strawberries) should be fresh, full fruits. Some types (e.g. raspberry and loganberry) are vulnerable to mould growth and need to be checked for this. All types need to be checked for damage and decay.
- *Stone fruits* (e.g. apricots, cherries, damsons, greengages, nectarines, peaches, plums) should be unblemished and without any bruising. Check that they are ripe without being too soft.
- *Avocado pears* should be ripe with a soft flesh but firm skin: test by pressing your thumb against the skin. A speckled, brown skin denotes over-ripe fruit.
- *Bananas* should be firm and unbruised. If green, they are under-ripe.
- *Grapes* (black or white) should be bunched, with no signs of decaying fruit.
- *Melons* should be heavy and firm without blemish or damage. Use your thumbs to test for ripeness at the flower end. Smell for evidence of scent.
- *Pineapple* should be firm with fresh leaves, not wilted, brown or dry. Check for damaged or very bruised areas on the fruit.
- *Rhubarb* should be pink to green in colour without too many leaves. Check that the stalk is not limp or discoloured.

Egg grading in the UK

Grade	Weight
Grade 1	70 g
Grade 2	65 g
Grade 3	60 g
Grade 4	55 g
Grade 5	50 g
Grade 6	45 g
Grade 7	under 45 g

Egg deliveries

Widely used in all aspects of food preparation, eggs need to be fresh, clean and undamaged. Many dishes use eggs as an ingredient and it is essential to keep a minimum stock to provide a continuous supply.

Those most commonly used are hen eggs, although duck, geese, plover and quail eggs are also available. Eggs are purchased by the case (360 eggs), half case (180 eggs), the dozen and half dozen.

Eggs can also be purchased as dried egg white, frozen pasteurised egg and spray dried egg. Used more in the bakery and confectionery trades, albumen substitutes are used for meringue and royal icing.

Eggs are a risk food and need careful handling and storage to prevent harmful bacterium developing such as Salmonella Enteriditis. When accepting a delivery of eggs, discard any cracked ones. Check more expensive eggs very carefully: duck and geese eggs can harbour bacteria. Only buy them from a supplier who is registered to sell such food items.

Check that eggs meet the quality points listed opposite

Key points when accepting egg deliveries

When buying or accepting a delivery of eggs, check for the following points:

- the shell of the egg should be clean and undamaged
- the white of the egg should be thick with a thin secondary white
- the yolk needs to be firm, domed and round with a rich yellow/orangey colour
- eggs should smell pleasant with no bad strong odour (hydrogen sulphide).

Bread and bread product deliveries

Traditionally bread was purchased sliced or unsliced or as whole items such as French sticks and roll products, and were purchased daily. Today bread items are also available par-baked, frozen ready to bake, and as gas-packed bake-off products.

When accepting bread for delivery, always check the date of the bread. Make sure that the packaging is not damaged and that no mould is evident on sliced bread. Many delivery people smoke and handle bread products without washing their hands; check that your suppliers have staff who are qualified to (at least) basic food hygiene standard and insist on a code of health and safety in the handling of bread food items.

Accepting bread deliveries

It is important to:

- order sufficient for daily use without running out
- ensure that the bread and bread products are fresh, not dry or hard
- freeze or dry excess bread to minimise cost and losses
- check *best before* dates and ensure stock rotation occurs.

Cake and biscuit deliveries

Cakes and biscuit products vary immensely in forms and packaging. They may come in tins, packets or boxes, or be delivered fresh, frozen or as convenience mixtures. The rotation and use of stock is essential to ensure efficient and effective use of these diverse foods.

Key points when accepting cake and biscuit deliveries
Check that:

- cakes and biscuits delivered are of the type, quantity and quality ordered
- packaging is not damaged
- the *best before* and *use by* dates have not been and will not be exceeded before the products are used
- frozen cakes are not defrosted or thawed prior to storage
- biscuit items are not damaged, crushed or stored in damp conditions.

Dairy food deliveries

High-protein foods present particular problems both in purchasing and storage. This food group presents the greatest risk of contamination through improper storage or handling once received into the store. It is very important for everyone involved in the handling of these foods to know the current legislation on their safe storage and use. Ignorance is no defence if someone is made ill by negligence or unprofessional practice. The caterer has a major responsibility to the public, as a large number of people may become ill very easily if you do not follow hygienic practices in dairy food storage.

When purchasing and accepting dairy food items for storage it is important to:

- check the *use by* date
- check that the *best before* and *use by* dates have not and will not be exceeded before the item is used
- order the minimum quantity to ensure freshness while ordering enough to cover your requirements
- check that all seals on milk, cream and soft cheese products are sound
- remember that meat or dairy items delivered after travelling on a warm van are dangerous and contravene the Food Hygiene (Amendment) Regulations, 1990
- store high risk foods (such as soft cheese, yoghurt or curd-based foods and dairy desserts with a pH value higher than 4.5) at a temperature below 5 °C (41 °F) or above 65 °C (149 °F) as appropriate
- check the goods delivered against the delivery note.

Accepting a delivery of dairy products

Dry goods deliveries

The correct storage and temperature conditions are essential for the short, medium and longer term storage of dry food items. It is essential that:

- dry food store shelving is at least 45 cm (18 in) off the floor
- food is not stored in contact with the floor
- dry stores are airy and well ventilated, with any windows covered by fly screens or mesh
- dry stores are fly and vermin proof
- there is adequate shelving and storage racks
- dry stores are cool and dry
- the stores are secured by lock, key or cage.

Dry goods in storage. Notice that heavier, canned products are stored below the softer, packaged products

- Look up the quality points for fresh meat in Unit 2D1 of the Cookery Units book. Draw up a chart for each meat type.
- Watch someone checking the packaging of delivered food items. Why is care needed?
- Ask your supervisor what you should do if fresh raw food is not fresh when delivered or does not meet with the purchasing specifications.
- Watch someone weighing fresh or frozen fish on delivery. How do they work out if the price per kilo is correct against the delivered amount of fish?

Temperatures of food on delivery

Your establishment will have laid down procedures for checking the temperatures of food on delivery. Make sure that you are familiar with these procedures and that you know what the temperature of each delivery item should be (these are given in *Types of food items and their storage*, pages 71–8).

The Department of Health produces leaflets outlining temperature controls for food delivery

Food delivery vehicles are subject to strict legislation, as given below. Note that the delivered food should also be at these temperatures when delivered.

- Delivery vehicles greater than 7.5 tonnes must be refrigerated to a temperature of less than 5 °C (41 °F) or above 63 °C (145 °F) from 1 April 1993.
- Delivery vehicles less than 7.5 tonnes are subject to different temperatures depending on the length of delivery time.
- For deliveries taking less than 12 hours, vehicles must be refrigerated to a temperature of less than 8 °C (46 °F) or above 63 °C (145 °F) from 1 April 1993.
- For deliveries taking longer than 12 hours, vehicles must be refrigerated to a temperature of less than 5–8 °C (41–46 °F) or above 63 °C (145 °F) from 1 April 1993.

Relevant food intended to be sold within two hours of preparation at 63 °C (145 °F) or within four hours of preparation below 63 °C (145 °F) is excluded.

Food companies today are more aware of the legislation regarding the delivery temperatures of food products. Ensure that you have a temperature probe to test the delivery temperature of food, especially high risk foods.

Deliveries of high risk foods

Food temperatures need to be checked carefully on delivery. Any food requiring refrigerated storage *should not be accepted* if the temperature is above 10 °C (50 °F). Any frozen food delivered at a temperature higher than 112 °C (234 °F) should also be rejected.

Always store refrigerated deliveries as soon as possible to avoid temperature rises in excess of the above stated temperatures.

Transferring food to stores

Once food is produced by the manufacturer, packaged and sent out to be delivered, there is a risk of mechanical damage to food items. All delivered foods need to be checked for crushed or damaged packaging, and then stored in such a way that damage will not occur during storage. Over-stacking cases or placing heavier loads onto weak packages will cause the foods to become crushed and spoiled.

When stacking a food trolley:

- check that all food items and products are placed carefully onto the trolley
- load the trolley with safety in mind; careless loading can cause damage to the food (through crushing or falling) or injury to someone near the trolley

- heavy sacks need to be transported on sack trucks, preferably the hydraulic type, to lift the heavy products such as bags of flour or potatoes
- load the heavier goods at the bottom of the trolley to avoid accidents, injuries and damage to the products
- make two lighter trips with food stores rather than one overloaded trip.

Types of food items and their storage

Ambient food storage

Dry or non-perishable food is stored at an ambient (or *room*) temperature; i.e. at the normal temperature and humidity of the environment. Each store area might have a varying ambient temperature and humidity level. One at approximately 50–60 per cent RH (Relative Humidity) is suitable as ambient storage. Coastal areas will have problems with ambient storage as the air humidity is high, being at sea level.

Certain food items benefit from dryer atmospheres. Dry herbs and spices can loose their qualities of flavour and aroma if stored in too dry an atmosphere, whereas biscuit and cereal products will retain their desirable dry texture.

Only a limited number of types of food items can be stored at ambient temperatures. This is because it can allow the development of harmful bacteria in high-risk, high-protein based food items, especially if these are left uncovered in ambient storage for an extended period of time before being chilled, refrigerated or frozen.

Chilled food storage

This type of storage is used for raw food such as meat, fish, dairy products and fish as temporary storage prior to preparation. It is also used for cooked and finished food items such as cooked egg based desserts, fresh cream products, cold savouries, salads, cold meats and starters.

Wrapped, packed and trayed meat in chilled storage

Remember the following points:

- chilled foods should only be held for the minimum time and used as soon after preparation as is possible. High-protein, dairy and high-risk products need to be managed carefully to avoid a build-up of too large a stock of chilled items. There is often a tendency to mix foods in chilled storage: this should be avoided
- always use an efficient stock rotation system to prevent foods being used in a stale state through neglect
- chilled food cabinets need to be cleaned daily and sited according to the manufacturer's instructions. Maintaining a free flow of cool air is essential to keep all food chilled at the correct temperature (usually 1–4 °C/34–39 °F). Chilled food cabinets should not be situated in direct sunlight, near heating units or under high-intensity lights.

See also *Storing cooked foods,* on page 75.

Frozen storage

Frozen foods are now a mainstay in preservation processes used by caterers and the public. Freezer units are used to store a wide variety of food items in both large and small establishments.

It is important for anyone involved in a food chain that uses, stores or transports frozen food to be aware of all the necessary precautions. At each point of the chain everyone involved needs to work effectively to reduce waste, make sure stock is rotated correctly and ensure that food packaging is added and handled in such a way that the products can be frozen and kept frozen safely. This is essential to ensure that the food is safe to eat when cooked, reheated or served cold.

Freezing food will not improve the quality of any food. Blast-freezers (which freeze quickly) are more effective than general freezers as the slower the process, the more liquid is lost from the food cells. This means that as food defrosts, the lost liquid will not return to the food cells, and the thawed food will be dryer than before it was frozen. Blast-freezers work in such a way that less liquid is drawn from the cells, and the food is therefore in a better condition when thawed.

See also Unit 2D16: *Preparing cook-freeze food* in the Cookery Units book.

The packaging of foods will affect the freezing of both the food itself and those foods stored near packaged products. For example, boxes of sheet puff pastry can act as an insulator to prevent foods trapped underneath from freezing. Careful attention must be paid to the method of stacking and packaging food items to be frozen. Never place warm or hot foods into freezer units.

A common problem with freezer storage is that food at the back or base of freezers can become ignored until freezer burn develops and the food has to be discarded. Efficient rotation of stock is essential.

Accepting deliveries of frozen foods
When accepting frozen food in deliveries, check that there is no ice build-up on the packaging. This can indicate that the freezing temperatures have fluctuated whilst the food item has been in a freezer: these items need to be rejected.

Quality frozen packed foods will have a light frost but not icy build-up of frozen water/moisture on the packaging. Check that all ice cream products are frozen hard on delivery and always store ice cream products in a separate freezer unit.

A modern 'walk-in' freezer storage unit

Food suitable for frozen storage
Almost all food can be frozen and stored for up to three months depending on the type of food and freezer unit being used. Meat, poultry, fish, vegetables, sauces, dough products, pastry goods and ice creams through to finished *à la carte* ready meals all find a place in the modern domestic and commercial freezer unit. The list of foods that can be frozen is almost endless; the most notable foods that can *not* be frozen include: salad vegetables, single cream, eggs, bananas and non-homogenised milk.

All frozen foods should be used within the time specified by the manufacturer.

Storage times and temperatures for freezers
The following symbols are used on the packaging of frozen products to indicate at what temperature and for how long they may be safely stored:

- * not above −6 °C/21 °F (for seven days)
- ** not above −12 °C/10 °F (for one month)
- *** not above −18 °C/0 °F (for three months)
- **** not above −18 °C/0 °F to −25 °C/ −13 °F (for three months or longer).

Frozen products must be stored at the following temperatures:

Ice cream	−22 °C/−8 °F to −18 °C/0 °F
Meat and fish	−20 °C/−4 °F to −16 °C/3 °F
Frozen foods	−20 °C/−4 °F to −16 °C/3 °F.

Thawing frozen food

Defrosting of frozen food can and often does lead to food poisoning due to a lack of knowledge, incompetent management or inadequate storage equipment.

The following guidelines may be helpful when defrosting food:

- thin, small or pre-portioned food items can be cooked from their frozen state
- small frozen food items should be defrosted in the refrigerator
- large joints of meat, game or poultry need to be hygienically defrosted before being cooked. Read the manufacturer's instructions for defrosting the frozen food item and follow this exactly. Frozen poultry and turkeys or meat joints that are cooked while the centre is still frozen are likely to cause food poisoning, as the cooking process will melt the icy centre while cooking the outside and encourage the growth of harmful bacteria
- thawing of turkey in particular needs to be managed professionally. A 9 kg (20 lb) oven-ready turkey can take 30 hours at ambient room temperature (10 °C/50 °F) to defrost. (See also *Thawing poultry* below.)
- food must be removed in good time from the freezer to allow for natural thawing to occur
- always wash your hands after handling frozen produce.

Thawing poultry

Frozen poultry present the most risk if not defrosted correctly.

It is important to:

- remove any plastic wrapping around frozen poultry, ducks or guinea fowl before thawing
- thaw completely in a cool room at a temperature of 10–15 °C (50–59 °F); never at a temperature higher than 15 °C (59 °F). Cool clean running water can be used as a method of thawing rather than a warm kitchen environment
- ensure the flesh is pliable and there is no ice remaining in the body cavity
- always cook the thawed poultry within 24 hours of thawing it
- cook the poultry *thoroughly* until the juices from the leg run clear
- refrigerate the cooked bird within 90 minutes of cooking or cooling (whichever is the sooner).

Storing cooked foods

Cooked foods should be kept in separate refrigeration or storage and away from uncooked food. If raw and cooked foods have to be stored in the same refrigerator, store raw foods at the bottom and cooked foods at the top. This prevents juices from raw meats contaminating cooked foods which may not need further cooking.

Cooked food items need to be cooled quickly and stored in a refrigerator when cool. Cooked pies, pasties and sausage rolls must be stored in a refrigerator at 7 °C (44 °F) with good air movement to keep the pastry dry and crisp. Pies containing gelatine, such as game or pork pies, should be stored below 5 °C (41 °F). Pasty pastry will become waxy and damp if stored in cold/high humidity conditions.

Food is kept in a *chilled* condition when stored at a temperature range from ambient temperature down to just above freezing point, i.e. 1–5 °C (34–41 °F). The food items are stored at this low temperature (usually 3 °C/38 °F) to preserve them for a short period of time (up to five days). Blast chiller machines may be used to chill cooked food down to the correct temperature for storage. *Never re-chill food that has already been chilled unless it has been safely cooked from its raw chilled state.* Note that cold chilling of foods and chilled storage is carried out to delay or slow down the decay and decomposition of food; it does not stop it completely.

Chill cabinets and units should be checked regularly. Temperature recordings should be taken twice daily with a thermometer and probe used in conjunction with sterile wipes (to prevent cross-contamination occurring). All temperature checks need to be recorded in a log.

Cook-chill is a food production system using conventional production methods but where foods are chilled rapidly (within 90 minutes) and stored at 3 °C (38 °F) for up to 5 days. See Unit 2D15: *Preparing cook-chill food* in the Cookery Units book.

Storage temperatures: cooked food

All the cooked food items listed below are subject to the Food Hygiene (Amendment) Regulations, 1990 (SI,1990 No 1431) and must be stored at a maximum storage temperature of 8 °C (46 °F).

Meat
Any cooked meat items or items containing cooked meat or meat substitutes which are intended for consumption without further reheating; cold cooked meats; meat removed from the can; meat and fish pâté; scotch eggs; pork pies with gelatine added after cooking; smoked or cured meat when cut/sliced after smoking or

curing (such as cured cooked hams, salamis and other fermented sausages). Also cooked meat items that are intended for further heating (e.g. meat pies, sausage rolls and ready meals).

Fish
Any cooked fish items or items containing cooked fish which are intended for consumption without further reheating; smoked or cured fish whether whole or cut after smoking or curing; cooked pies containing fish (or fish substitute).

Eggs
Any cooked eggs or items containing cooked eggs which are intended for consumption without further reheating; quiches.

Cereals, pulses, pasta
Any cooked cereal or pulse items or items containing cooked cereals or pulses which are intended for consumption without further reheating; fresh pasta with meat or fish fillings (e.g. ravioli).

Dairy products
Cheese; dairy based desserts with a pH value of 4.5 or more (such as trifles, creme caramels, whipped cream desserts); dairy cream cakes; or any food item containing egg or milk added before baking.

Vegetables
Cooked vegetables; salads, especially prepared vegetable salads containing high risk relevant foods (such as pasta salad); pies or pasties containing vegetables.

Dough products
Dough products containing meat, fish or their substitutes.

Sandwiches
Any sandwich fillings containing meat, fish or eggs, e.g. chicken, egg mayonnaise or tuna; any sandwiches, filled rolls and bread products containing soft cheese, smoked or cured fish or meat, or cooked products which are not intended to be sold within 24 hours.

Sandwiches containing any other relevant foods and any sandwich intended to be sold within 4 to 24 hours of preparation must be stored at this temperature, but any sandwich intended to be sold within 4 hours of preparation are not covered by legislation.

Storing uncooked food items

Uncooked food needs to be checked on delivery and stored according to its food type. We have covered the storage of many of the uncooked foods in each food type under the sections above (see *Ambient food storage, Chilled food storage* and *Frozen storage* on pages 71–3).

Use common sense to identify which uncooked foods are risk foods. Notice how uncooked food items look and smell. This enables you to carry out a rapid assessment of the food (and is known as *organoleptic assessment*). Remember the rule: *when in doubt, check it out.* If you are uncertain, always confirm your suspicions with a senior member of staff; never assume responsibility where uncooked food may have been contaminated by prolonged or improper storage. Never accept food you believe to be inferior or unfit for human consumption.

Never store uncooked and cooked food together if it can be avoided. If you must store uncooked food with cooked food, store the uncooked *below* the cooked food in a refrigerator or cold room. Keep uncooked foods away from the walls of cold storage rooms, refrigerators and chill boxes.

Preserved food

Preserved foods have been used for hundreds if not thousands of years, where food was salted or dried to prevent deterioration before the invention of the refrigerator. *Preserved foods* covers a wide range of food types, and here we will look at those most commonly purchased for food storage and subsequent use.

Food preservation is the treatment of food to delay, prevent or inhibit spoilage and pathogenic (disease carrying) organisms from growing, resulting in food being unfit for human consumption. There are six types of food preservation: low/high temperature; dehydration (moisture control); oxygen restriction (controlled atmosphere); smoking; irradiation; chemical.

Low temperature preservation
This preserves food by slowing down the speed of enzymic reactions within the food. It can be carried out *above freezing* (in a refrigerator), *at freezing point* (in chillers) and *below freezing* (in freezers).

Food preserved by low temperature should be stored according to type; i.e. chilled food should be stored as stated on page 71, and frozen food stored as stated on page 72.

High temperature preservation
This includes processes such as pasteurisation, sterilisation, Ultra Heat Treatment (UHT) and cooking.

Dehydration
Foods preserved by dehydration are dried out to below 25 per cent of their normal moisture content. This can be carried out by drying naturally under the sun, by artificial drying methods or by accelerated freeze-drying.

Many convenience foods are preserved by drying. When required for use, water is added to re-constitute the food item. All dried preserved foods need to be stored in a low relative humidity and kept dry, stored off the floor on racking or shelving. When dried foods are delivered, check any packages that have been damaged during transit or storage and look for mould growth on dry preserved foods kept for long period of time. Always consult the manufacturer's suggested *best before* date.

Chemical methods of preservation

The most commonly found chemical methods of preservation are carried out by salting, sugaring or curing processes. There are also several acid preservation methods.

Controlled atmosphere preservation

This method is known as *Modified Atmosphere Packaging* (MAP). It is becoming more widely used and many bread, salad and vegetable products are preserved using this method. Gas replaces most of the oxygen around the product to slow down spoilage and the packaging keeps the products in this atmosphere. These products still need to be preserved by using temperature control, so need to be stored in chillers and and refrigerated areas.

Smoking

Here food is pickled or brined and suspended over smouldering hardwood chips. The foods are partially dehydrated with a particular flavour and colour; cheese and fish are often smoked. Smoked products must still be refrigerated below 3 °C (37 °F) to prevent the development of *toxins* (poisonous substances).

Food irradiation

Here food is subjected to *ionising radiation* from gamma rays. Insects, parasites and most forms of microbes are destroyed but spores and toxins can remain. The Food (Control of Irradiation) Regulations, 1990 authorised the irradiation of food in the United Kingdom. Irradiation of food is subject to very strict licensing controls and all irradiated food must be labelled in accordance with The Food Labelling (Amendment) (Irradiated Food) Regulations, 1990. Foods commonly irradiated include fish, chicken, potatoes, onions, spices and strawberries.
When taking delivery of irradiated foods, accept and store as for other foods, after checking that they are clearly labelled *irradiated*.

To do

- Find out the minimum stock levels for dry food stores in your establishment.
- Check the freezers to see if they contain any food suffering from freezer burn.
- Find out if your establishment buys cook-chill food. If so, where and how is it stored?
- Find out how the stores person monitors and records food in the chest freezer, and how often this is carried out.

Receiving areas

These must be kept clean, tidy and free from rubbish at all times. They must also be secured against unauthorised access. Make sure you are familiar with all the security points given in Unit G1: *Maintaining a safe and secure environment* (pages 1–32).

Essential knowledge

Receiving areas should be secured from unauthorised access at all times in order to:
- reduce and prevent the risk of pilfering, stock shrinkage, damage or loss
- comply with food hygiene regulations
- ensure work is carried out efficiently and effectively.

Storage conditions

Lighting

Lighting of food storage and food areas in general tends to be overlooked, and may be inadequate. This can cause problems such as eye strain for people working in storage areas. Store rooms without natural light need adequate illumination to ensure floor spaces behind and under shelving can be seen easily for cleaning and carrying out infestation checks. Fluorescent lighting strips need to be protected by diffusers to prevent accidental breakage.

Corridors, walkways and secondary rooms need to be well lit to maintain a safe and secure working environment. Natural light and internal lighting should be balanced in kitchen areas to ensure comfortable vision during prolonged periods, as reflective glare can cause tiredness and fatigue.

Walk-in refrigerators and cold rooms should illuminate when their doors are opened to prevent accidents occurring. Basement or semi-basement kitchens and stores need particular types of lighting and it is essential to seek the advice of a specialist to obtain the correct type and strength of lighting, to ensure safe working conditions.

Kitchen fittings need to be placed with care to ensure effective illumination and ease of cleaning. Any lighting placed over stoves or moist cooking areas (such as bain-maries) will need to have watertight diffuser covers.

Always report any defects and problems with lighting immediately.

Ventilation

Good ventilation of stores and kitchen areas is essential to keep the *relative humidity* (RH) in balance for the types of foods being stored. It is also important to keep the kitchen area free from the build up of heat and steam which causes condensation, grease and the ideal conditions for contamination.

Working conditions can be seriously undermined by inadequate ventilation. Foods are greatly affected by ventilation and expert advice should be sought when deciding on type and positioning of ventilation systems. Natural ventilation often needs to be supported by mechanical venting systems to create a balanced flow of clean air in and poor air out; you would normally aim for 85 per cent input capacity to rated output capacity. Equipment producing steam and moisture needs to be covered by canopies and be directly extracted through piping. Extractors need to extract to an outside wall at a level where they will not pollute the air with food odour and dust (e.g. below the restaurant windows or guest accommodation).

Ducting (piping) filters need to be cleaned and their filters replaced regularly to prevent a build-up of grease and dust; this is a recognised fire hazard in food preparation and production areas. Poor ventilation not only reduces the shelf life of many dry stored foods but can damage your health.

Temperature monitoring

We have covered many of the important temperatures dealing with each food type, storage condition, methods of preservation and associated storage situations. Temperatures must always be monitored and recorded.

Temperature is clearly a key control factor in the storage of food and associated food items, to ensure:

- *quality food* for preparation and production
- *safe handling* from the delivery stage through to the finished dish
- *minimal food losses.*

The Food Hygiene (Amendment) Regulations, 1990 (SI. 1990 No. 1431)

It is important to read and be aware of this legislation when storing foods. The new regulations set out those food types which are subject to temperature control above 63 °C (145 °F) and below 8 °C (46 °F). Note that high risk relevant foods must be stored below 5 °C (41 °F), and other relevant food items (as detailed in the regulations) must be stored below 8 °C (46 °F).

- Milk and cream need to be stored below 5 °C (41 °F) as soon as delivered and received.
- Canned foods should be stored at ambient room temperature.
- Flour and cereals should be stored at ambient room temperature in containers with tight fitting lids. Flour should be stored off the ground and in dry conditions.
- Weekly inspections should be carried out to identify any insect infestation or rodent damage, the presence of weevils or any general damage due to improper storage.
- As a general rule for refrigerated foods, the closer the refrigerator operates to 1 °C (34 °F) the safer it is.

Temperature storage of ice cream

Ice cream is a high risk food and easily susceptible to bacterial growth, so needs careful handling during both storage and service.

Ideally a separate ice cream freezer should be used (larger food operations are often supplied with free freezer units by manufacturers). Within freezers, ice cream should be stored in storage tubs with tight fitting lids. It should never be stored with raw food commodities. Any thawed ice cream should be discarded immediately and not re-frozen or used in any other way.

Food operational areas where food is served are often warm, humid environments which can melt ice cream quickly. The operational storage temperature of ice cream needs to be −20 °C/−4 °F (long term) to −8 °C/18 °F (short term).

Maintaining stores in a clean condition

Cleaning is the systematic application of energy to a surface, substance or equipment with the aim of removing or preventing dirt. Unit 2D12: *Cleaning food production areas, equipment and utensils* (pages 99–110) covers this in detail.

All food storage areas must not only be cleaned, but kept clean on a consistent and regular basis. Rigorous inspection by Government Health Officers has resulted in the closure of many unprofessional food operators. However, many working kitchens may still employ staff who would benefit from training in hygiene management at basic, intermediate and advanced levels.

If you are involved in the handling, preparation or sale of food to customers, you must take responsibility to improve the standards of cleanliness in your workplace. Stores need to be cleaned daily and weekly with a monthly *deep clean* to ensure safe and hygienic storage of food items. Daily checks should be carried out to keep a check on infestation, contamination and general cleanliness of delivery and storage areas.

The packaging, shelving, storage bins, refrigerators and freezers need to be cleaned weekly to prevent the build up of ice or risk of contamination from raw food juices and debris. Shelves need to be cleaned regularly; make sure you remove any bottles, jars or containers to clean away any dust and debris underneath or behind them. Keep waste bins and refuse areas clean, and always replace any bin lids after use.

Always and consistently ensure that if you need to touch your head in any way, you wash your hands afterwards. Notice what habits you have developed; any unhygienic ones will need to be addressed to improve the qualitative handling of food from its arrival at the stores to the finished dish.

To do

- Draw up a plan of the ventilation systems used in your stores to keep ambient and humid atmospheres balanced.
- Find out what cleaning schedule is used in your storage and kitchen areas.
- Check the lighting in your stores. Can you see clearly enough to check for cleanliness and possible infestation?
- Check the temperatures of two types of store. Do they comply with regulations?

Types of food packaging

Packaging serves the purpose of assisting in the preservation of food. It protects against water vapour, light, dust, oxygen, dirt, weight loss, mechanical damage and the infestation of insects and micro-organisms. Packaging materials must always be sterile to prevent the risk of contamination through *pathogens* (disease-carrying agents).

The most common forms of packaging are: cans, bottles or jars, packets or boxes and bags or sacks. The packaging itself is normally made from: plastic (rigid or flexible), glass, cardboard, paper, foil or tin.

Cans

We use a large variety of canned foods, ranging across fruits and fruit juices, purées, vegetables and their concentrates, condensed milk, jams, baked beans, canned cooked meats, patés and tins of powdered soups, sauces and stocks.

Canned food usually contains salt or sugared liquid solutions which preserve the food item. The risk of contamination from canned food today is low. However, reactions can occur inside canned food which cause a build up of gas. This causes the top of the can to *bulge;* any cans like this should be discarded. Always check before accepting canned foods that the cans are sound, undamaged and not bulged. Look for signs of age: the boxes containing the canned food should be clean, unbroken and coded.

Do not store canned goods in high or humid temperatures, as this can damage the tin seal (through internal corrosion). The tin would become rusty, and in an extreme case, would develop pinholes. This in turn would lead to food becoming contaminated and unfit for human consumption.

High acid foods (such as fruit) are subject to bulging or blowing if stored longer than advised by the manufacturer. Tins of ham, tongue or other processed meats should be stored in a dry goods store and chilled prior to use for ease of slicing.

Opened canned products should be placed in a suitable covered container made from stainless steel, glass or plastic (*never* aluminium) and kept refrigerated. When opening a can, always inspect the contents. Use smell and taste to confirm that the food is fresh and untainted by metal or fermentation.

Canned food can be stored for up to five years depending on the type of food. Always follow the recommended storage time of the manufacturer.

Bottles or jars

Food delivered and accepted in jars or bottles includes milk, fruit, jams, pickles and dressings. The bottle should not be cracked or chipped, but sound and sealed. Check that the lid seal has not been broken or damaged: if so, these items should be rejected upon delivery. Store them where damage is unlikely to occur and away from strong sunlight, which can trigger the production of gases, fermentation and spoilage.

Keep opened bottles and jars in the refrigerator. Never wash out and re-use milk bottles for storing food or re-use jars that are not sterile.

Left: bottle and jar storage. Right: packet storage

Packets or boxes

Food delivered in packets or boxes should be undamaged and tally with the order sheet and delivery note. Always check for signs of aging. Torn or crushed packaging may indicate that the seal of dried foods has become damaged and the food may have become contaminated.

Check the delivery carton for signs of leaking packets. Be aware of possible infestation from cockroaches, silverfish or other insects and check for vermin damage. Some deliveries are badly handled, and boxes may be crushed by over-stacking. When the delivery arrives, count the goods in and check each carton, package or box with the driver to make sure the delivery is complete and that goods are stacked correctly.

Cereals and dry goods should be sealed. If you find any split or ripped packaging, notify the person making the delivery and ensure that a credit note is issued by the supplier. Check the *use by* date suggested by the manufacturer and rotate stock so that all goods are used before this date.

Bags or sacks

Bulk foods are delivered in bags or sacks. Food items that might be delivered in bags or sacks include: flour, cereals, pulses, dry pre-mixes and specialist additives. On delivery, check for signs of vermin attack (i.e. nibbled or gnawed edges). Do not accept any damp, stained, damaged or cut sacks. Bags should always be sealed: if any are delivered with a damaged seal or open, reject them immediately.

Stacked potatoes

If infestation is found, seal the unit in a secure plastic bag or liner, move the food away from other food stores and inform the suppliers. If they are not forthcoming, inform your environmental health officer: this ensures the supplier conforms to their responsibilities.

Always store sacks or bags of food on pallets off the floor surface. Use effective stock rotation methods and mark the delivery date on each sack or bag using a pen. Check that you know which bag of flour is which, as many are not labelled to indicate whether they are plain, strong, soft or self-raising.

What have you learned?

1 Why should receiving areas be secured from unauthorised areas at all times?

2 Why must deliveries tally with both the order and delivery documentation?

3 What should you do if certain items are missing from the delivery?

4 What is *ambient* storage?

5 Why is temperature important when receiving delivery of food items?

6 What should you do when accepting delivery of fish?

ELEMENT 2: Maintaining food stores

Stock rotation and storage systems

You can ensure that food is stored in a safe and hygienic manner together with effective and efficient stock rotation by using a simple system supported by modern equipment, i.e. shelving, racking, storage bins, etc.

Racking within stores should be mobile in order to make the best use of the space available and make the area easy to clean. You should be able to inspect all stored food easily, without having to move large volumes of heavy food. This is also essential in order to be able to check effectively for infestation, contamination and any general repairs that may be necessary on walls, flooring, etc.

A stock rotation system is essential in order to ensure that older foods are used before newer purchases. Remember the rule: *first in, first out.* All foods are subject to rotation, so the system must run across all types of stores.

Keep the following points in mind:

- the method of rotation needs to be simple, so that regular checks can be made on stock levels. Fresh and perishable foods will need to be checked daily for condition and *best before* dates
- careful purchasing and stock rotation will help prevent over-ordering of stock, which results in food remaining in storage for longer than necessary
- remember that extended storage can lead to problems such as moulds developing on food (especially in stores with inadequate ventilation) and foods being attacked by rodents or infestation, becoming unfit to eat
- if food is stored incorrectly let your superior know. If food is damaged on delivery and still being accepted, ensure that it is brought to someone's attention.

Essential knowledge

A constant stock of food items should be maintained in order to:

- ensure that food supplies are available at the time of request so that preparation and production can continue to meet customer demand
- sustain the food quality and standards by ensuring no individual food item is out of stock, unless supplies can not be secured due to bad weather, crop failure or other unforeseen circumstance.

Essential knowledge

Correct storage and rotation procedures should be followed in order to:

- maintain stock in a useable condition. Stock stored incorrectly will suffer damage and a reduced shelf life and this can reduce profits
- ensure that *sell by* dates are not exceeded. These dates provide a guide to the shelf life of stored products, and if these are exceeded the food may become unfit for consumption or inferior in quality. This could taint the flavour and affect the texture or appearance of certain food items.

Keeping stock records

All stock must be monitored both to maintain stock levels and to ensure that stock is not being stolen or lost. You will need to keep records both of stock held and stock issued. Keep all stock records up to date, and keep all delivery notes, order sheets and invoices in a safe place. Never rely on others: make certain that paperwork is managed correctly.

Record information clearly and accurately. Use only metric units for all foods, in line with the rest of Europe. Keep dry goods together in a logical order, with tally bin cards to assist in stock taking.

To do

- Find out what method of stock rotation is used in your stores.
- Look at the reporting procedures for your establishment in cases of stock shrinkage, pilfering, loss or damage. Do you have an effective documentation system for each store area? Can information be easily accessed?
- Find out what measures are taken in your stores area to prevent unauthorised access.
- Find out how VAT and credit notes are dealt with by the stores person.

Maintaining storage areas

All storage areas must be kept clean, tidy and free from rubbish. They should also be protected against unauthorised access in order to prevent loss or damage to stored goods, to prevent food from being removed with documentation and to prevent stock being removed in the incorrect order (i.e. not in line with the stock rotation system in use). If a stores areas has been broken into or food items appear to be missing, report the situation to your supervisor as soon as possible. They will decide what further action (such as calling the police) should be taken.

If you spot an intruder within a stores area, do not approach them alone. Report the matter to your supervisor, or seek assistance from other staff. Make sure that you are familiar with the relevant safety and security points given in Unit G1: *Maintaining a safe and secure environment* (pages 26–7).

Essential knowledge

Storage areas should be secured from unauthorised access at all times in order to:

- reduce and prevent the risk of pilfering, stock shrinkage, damage or loss
- comply with food hygiene regulations
- prevent temperature changes in controlled temperature environments
- ensure work is carried out efficiently and effectively.

Storing meat and poultry

Raw meat and poultry should be stored in separate refrigerators at temperatures between –1 °C (30 °F) and 1 °C (34 °F). The relative humidity should be approximately 90 per cent. Any humidity level above 95 per cent will create microbial growth, while any humidity level below 85 per cent will cause evaporation and therefore weight loss.

- Stored raw meat and poultry should not touch the wall surface of the refrigerator or cool room.
- Raw, fresh meat joints should be hung on hooks in a cool room between –1 °C (12 °F) and 1 °C (34 °F), with drip trays placed under the meat to collect any blood.
- Cuts of meat should be wrapped in lightly oiled greaseproof paper and kept on a clean tray until required. Delivered meat cuts should not be stored in the packaging they were delivered in: small joints and whole cuts should be wiped with a damp cloth and wrapped as stated above.

Trayed, prepared meat storage

Beef usually has a longer shelf life than lamb, pork or poultry. Processed raw meats (such as sausages) have the shortest shelf life and need careful stock rotation management to prevent contamination occurring.

Raw foods should always be kept separate from cooked foods during storage, unless only one refrigerator unit is available. If this is the case, tray and store all cooked foods at the top of the refrigerator and all raw meats at the bottom to prevent juices from the raw meat contaminating the cooked meats which may not be reheated. Meat of different types should not be stored together on the same tray. Clean and replace drip trays and trays used for cuts of meat daily, otherwise blood juices will break down and contaminate the meat. This will cause rancidity and a bad odour to develop and the meat will eventually need to be discarded.

Safe storage times under hygienic conditions for raw meats at –1 °C (12 °F) are as follows:

- Beef 3 weeks
- Veal 1–3 weeks
- Lamb 1–2 weeks
- Pork 1–2 weeks
- Edible offal 4 days.

When preparing meat in the storage area to send to the kitchen, use separate preparation tables and boards to prevent cross-contamination occurring between raw and cooked meats. Always wash your hands after handling meat and between handling either different types of meat or raw and cooked meats. Consistency is sometimes difficult to maintain, especially when you are busy, but you should never compromise on safety.

Raw meat should be kept refrigerated until required. If raw meat is cleaned with cold water it must either be dried thoroughly or used within 24 hours. If you return wet meat to the refrigerator it will break down very quickly, becoming sour and unfit to eat.

Storing fish

Commercial refrigerators always used to have a separate draw for fish storage, where trays would hold the fish packed in ice until required. Today, however, many smaller food operations do not have special fish storage units but use standard refrigeration.

When storing fish, keep the following points in mind:

- fish should ideally be stored in ice in a fish refrigerator or at the base of a refrigerator operating at –1 °C (30 °F) to 1 °C (34 °F), covered and on trays which are cleaned and changed daily
- frozen fish should be delivered and stored at –18 °C (0 °F)
- use all fresh fish or thawed frozen fish within 2 days

- never re-freeze any fish that has previously been frozen
- keep smoked fish separate from fresh or frozen fish to avoid tainting other fish products. Smoked fish has a strong flavour which can taint white fish especially very easily. Wrap any smoked fish in a lightly oiled paper to prevent it from drying out.

Storing vegetables

Onions racked for storage

Root vegetables

Root vegetables should be stored in bins or racks. Always remove them from the delivery sack or bag to make the vegetables visible. Open up any coloured netting which can disguise the true appearance of carrots, swedes or parsnips. Stacking of root vegetables causes sweating and rot to set in; keep them well ventilated.

Potatoes

Storage needs to be in a low humidity to prevent condensation. Delivered in 25 kg (55 lb) brown paper sacks, potatoes should be kept in a cool dark store, away from strong sunlight. Light causes the potatoes to turn green and become hard; they can also become poisonous.

Avoid stacking sacks of potato and keep stock rotation accurate by marking the delivery date on each sack.

Bulbs

Leeks, onions, shallots and garlic should be stored in a low humidity to prevent condensation which can cause damage and spoilage. Carry out careful checks every day on the condition of bags of onions and shallots, removing any soft or decaying products to minimise spoilage of batch storage.

Leaves

Cabbages, endives, spinach, watercress, lettuce, corn salad, kale and Brussels sprouts tops require cool storage with minimal handling to prevent damage to leaves. Green vegetables need to be stored on well-ventilated racking, with salad leaves in a cool store kept in their delivery packaging. Green vegetables should be crisp and bright in colour without signs of leaf decay or wilted appearance.

Flowers

Broccoli, cauliflower, globe artichokes and calabrese should be stored in a cool place with a low humidity. Do not stack boxes or trays of flower vegetables as this causes bruising and sweating, resulting in decomposition. Avoid prolonged storage of these items: order in line with need.

Fruit vegetables

Courgettes, marrows, aubergines, peppers, avocado pears, cucumbers, gherkins and pumpkins require a storage temperature of 4–7 °C (40–45 °F). Store them in a cool room or refrigerator on trays or in their delivery box, being careful not to stack or crush the vegetables.

Seed and stem vegetables
Peas, beans, asparagus, celery and endive tend to be purchased frozen or fresh when in season. Store stem and seed vegetables in cool dry conditions; some are damaged by condensation.

Fungi
Mushrooms, ceps, morels and chanterelles are best stored in their delivery container in a cool room. Many edible fungi are costly and need careful handling to prevent damage. Never stack units of mushrooms or special fungi. Store at approximately 4–6 °C (40–43 °F): fungi are damaged by temperatures lower than this. Order in line with need; if you have over-ordered, excess fungi can be pickled or dried to prevent wastage.

Storing eggs

Eggs should be stored in a refrigerator at 1–4 °C (34–40 °F). They will take on the odour from any strong smelling foods around them because of their porous shell, so store them away from strong smelling foods. Eggs are a risk food and need careful handling and storage to prevent harmful bacterium developing such as Salmonella Enteriditis.

Storing bread items

Fresh bread should be stored in a well-ventilated room. Arrange it in such a way that it will be used according to when it was ordered, ensuring stock rotation. Any gas-packed bread can be stored in ambient storage providing the packaging has not been damaged in any way. Frozen bread items that are ready to bake should be stored in freezers at –18 °C (0 °F) and used according to the manufacturer's instructions.

Bread wrapped and racked for storage

Freshly purchased bread items will last for up to four days if stored in the correct conditions. Always check the *use by* date. If you are left with stale bread, it can be dried and used for bread-crumbs or rusks, bread puddings or croutons, or soaked to add bulk to stuffings. Rolls need to be used within 24 hours or frozen after 12 hours and used within one month of freezing to maintain some freshness. Note that frozen bread items tend to be dry once thawed unless they are served hot.

Storing cakes and biscuits

Cakes and biscuits cover an enormous range of products, needing a variety of storage conditions.

Dry cake and biscuit products such as sponges and sweet or savoury biscuits should be stored in dry storage at a temperature of 5–10 °C (41–50 °F). Cake mixtures that are powder based (convenience) should be stored at least 45 cm (18 in) off the floor in the dry food storage area.

Cakes and biscuits wrapped and racked for storage

Moist cakes finished or filled with buttercream, sugar-based fillings, fudge icing, etc. need to be kept cool. Any cakes or biscuits containing cream or cream products must be refrigerated at a temperature below 5 °C (41 °F) to prevent contamination and spoilage. Frozen cakes need to be defrosted in the refrigerator, *not* in ambient conditions.

Storing cakes and biscuits is made simple by following the storage instructions on the packaging for each individual food item. Never over-order in this area as many cake and biscuit products have a short shelf life. Use them in strict stock rotation and keep a log of the *use by* dates for each range of cake or biscuit food.

Storing dairy foods

Dairy foods such as milk and cream are ideal foods for bacterial growth. As soon as dairy foods (and imitation cream) are delivered they should be refrigerated. All cheese needs to be wrapped or contained to prevent being tainted by other foods.

Chilled storage of dairy products

Check the packaging of any dairy food items on delivery: cartons may have developed leaks or bottle tops may have been damaged by birds. The packaging may have suffered damage due to poor storage during transportation, and may, in some cases, have been penetrated.

Place any butter and cheese in the refrigerator at a temperature below 5 °C (41 °F). Remember that the quality of cheese is affected by prolonged storage: it develops a soft, stodgy texture. Never store crates of milk below fresh meat which might drip juices on to the milk, resulting in contamination.

The rotation of dairy food commodities is essential to ensure that dairy products are fresh at the time of preparation and production. Always check the *use by* date. Dairy foods part-used and returned to the refrigerator need to be sealed or covered to prevent contamination.

Storing dry goods

Dry goods, as the name implies, covers all those foods of a dry nature, including foods that are tinned or packaged. The range includes sugars, pulses, cereals, flour, spices and herbs, jams and pickles, condiments, bottled foods, canned and tinned foods, bread, cakes and biscuits. Areas used for the storage of dry food commodities need to be cool, well ventilated and lit with a relative humidity of R.H. 60–65 per cent (see *Ambient storage*, page 71). Make sure there is enough space to store single or multi-pack dry food items, so that effective stock rotation can be carried out.

Dry goods need to be stored off the floor or in storage bins which can be sealed. Tinned goods need to be stored in cases or as individual units depending on the unit of issue or use. When tins or cans are delivered, check that they are not bulged or damaged and look for leaks or staining on the box.

Dry goods storage

Use all goods in strict rotation; remember the rules: *first in – first out* and *last in – last out.* The effective storage of dry goods revolves around the method of stock rotation used. Always know the volume of dry stores needed to sustain supply to the various catering operations. Store each dry food commodity in the best conditions given the availability and design of the storage space. Some catering operations have purpose-built rooms, while many have only a cupboard or small room. The essential point is to keep the dry store clean, tidy and well ventilated. Keep strong smelling foods separate from more delicate foods and *never* store cleaning materials with dry food products.

To do

- Find out how dairy products are stored in your kitchen. Check the temperature of the refrigerated units.
- Find out where meat joints are hung for storage. How long are they hung for? At what temperature?
- Watch a delivery of fresh poultry. Notice how quickly the food is moved into storage and how it is stored.
- Make a list of the storage temperatures for high risk foods.
- Check all the stores to see if any food items seem to be stored incorrectly. Make a list of any that you think may need to be moved and talk to your supervisor about the list.
- Find out whether your establishment uses any vacuum packed foods. If so, where are these stored?
- Find out where eggs are stored in your kitchen. Are they in the best storage space available?

Health, safety and hygiene

Note all points given in Unit G1: *Maintaining a safe and secure environment* (pages 1–32) concerning general attention to health, safety and hygiene.

When accepting and storing food deliveries the following points are particularly important:

- high risk and high protein food must be stored in accordance with the Food Hygiene (Amendment) Act 1990
- foods that are damaged, contaminated or infested must be returned to the supplier immediately
- receiving areas must be kept free from rubbish and kept clean and tidy at all times
- any spillages should be wiped up as soon as they occur
- food should be stacked in a safe and appropriate manner, avoiding the risk of injury to yourself or colleagues and preventing damage to the food items
- each store area should be cleaned regularly as part of an overall cleaning policy
- cleaning materials must always be stored away from food items.

Essential knowledge

The main contamination threats when accepting food deliveries and maintaining the food store are as follows:

- infestation; introduced either through packaging of deliveries, poor building maintenance or ineffective cleaning schedules
- rodent infestation; mice or rats coming into contact with foods left uncovered. Sacks and bags should be stored in bins with tight fitting lids or off the floor on racking or pallet trays
- insects contaminating food; house flies, cockroaches, silver fish or beetles coming into contact with food. Fly screens should be fitted to windows
- cross-contamination; occurring between cooked and uncooked food during storage
- food poisoning bacteria passed among foods and equipment; caused by using the same preparation areas, equipment and utensils for handling cooked and raw, uncooked high risk and high protein foods
- food poisoning bacteria passed from humans to food; from open cuts, sores, sneezing, colds, sore throats or dirty hands to food
- food poisoning bacteria passed through dirty equipment; caused by using unclean, unhygienic equipment: utensils and tables, trays, preparation sinks and preparation areas
- contamination through products being left opened or uncovered; foreign bodies can fall into mixes and uncovered sacks, bags, jars or tins
- incorrect waste disposal.

Planning your time

Refer to *Planning your time* in the Cookery Units book (pages 1–4) concerning general points that you should always be aware of when working in a food storage area.

When accepting deliveries and maintaining a food store, the following points are especially important to remember:

- tally food delivered, checking that the order and delivery notes match and that all items are undamaged and of the quality and quantity ordered
- plan your work efficiently and effectively to ensure consistent supply of food and related food items for preparation and production in line with daily schedules
- work in a clean and organised manner attending to any priorities and laid down procedures.

To do

- Is the storage space available being used to full potential in your kitchen?
- Identify any safety hazards within your stores that need addressing.
- Check whether your store is equipped with two sinks for food handling.
- Find out what measures your establishment takes to prevent infestation in storage areas.
- Make sure that cleaning materials are not stored in the same room as food items in any storage area.
- Look for signs of infestation in dry stores and store rooms. What might raise your suspicions?

Disposing of waste

- Always dispose of waste in the correct manner according to laid down procedures, meeting adequate hygiene standards.
- Clean up after yourself as you work, disposing of waste materials cleanly and efficiently, to prevent contamination of uncooked and cooked food items and ingredients to prevent health hazards.
- Keep storage areas clean and tidy, free from any build-up of waste packaging and general rubbish. This helps to prevent accidents and the risk of contamination or infestation.

Dealing with unexpected situations

While working within the stores, you may discover one of the following:

- theft
- contaminated food
- infestation
- a potential hazard (such as defective equipment)
- an intruder.

When dealing with these unexpected situations, remain calm and act in a rational manner. *Never put yourself or others at risk.* Seek advice from your supervisor, manager or a senior member of staff. If you are advised to say nothing about some form of contamination threat (e.g. pest infestation), seek advice from the local Environmental Health Office.

What have you learned?

1 Why should storage areas be secured from unauthorised access at all times?

____

____

____

____

2 Why do you need to maintain a constant stock of food items?

____

____

____

____

3 Why is it essential to follow correct storage and rotation procedures?

____

____

____

____

4 How should you store meat after delivery?

____

____

____

5 What kinds of contamination threats should you be aware of when working in the stores area?

____

____

____

____

Extend your knowledge

1 Look at different systems of stock control, stock management, quality assurance systems and methods. Visit other catering establishments to examine the type of food storage used; can any elements of their system be adopted and adapted for your own food storage system?
2 Look at stores ledgers and record keeping. How might a minimum and maximum stock record card system improve the management of food storage, stock rotation and general food control?
3 Look at the financial implications of theft, holding dead stock, and bulk purchasing. Investigate how security can be improved to prevent pilfering.
4 Find out which food types do not have purchasing specifications and why this is the case.
5 Search business directories for alternative suppliers. Request price lists and account sale requirements and conditions. How do they compare with your present suppliers?
6 Find out how to take a stock check, both speculatively and as a method of checking for pilfering or for monthly for audit purposes.
7 Investigate different computer based food stock control systems. How do they work? Are they user friendly? How much does the software and hardware cost?

UNIT 2D12

Cleaning food production areas, equipment and utensils

ELEMENTS 1, 2 AND 3: Cleaning food production areas, equipment and utensils

What do you have to do?

- Check that sinks, wash basins, drains, gullies, traps and overflows are clean, free-flowing and satisfy food hygiene regulations. Clean them as necessary.
- Check that floors and walls are clean and satisfy health, safety and food hygiene regulations. Clean them as necessary.
- Check that all food production equipment is turned off and dismantled before cleaning.
- Clean food production equipment correctly then store it appropriately.
- Check that shelving, cupboards and drawers are clean and tidy, and satisfy health, safety and hygiene regulations. Clean them as necesary.
- Clean food production utensils correctly; check that they are dry, clean, free from damage and then store them appropriately.
- Leave any cleaning equipment used in a clean and tidy state and stored correctly.
- Handle and dispose of waste correctly.

What do you need to know?

- The reasons for cleaning.
- How to plan your time efficiently, taking care of priorities and any laid down procedures.
- Why equipment is turned off and dismantled before cleaning.
- How to deal with unexpected situations.
- Why waste must be handled and disposed of correctly.
- Which type of cleaning equipment and materials to use in food production areas and on equipment and utensils.

What is *cleaning?*

Cleaning is the removal of all food residues and any dirt or grease that may have become attached to work surfaces, equipment and utensils during the preparation and cooking of food.

To clean effectively, we need to use *energy*. This can be in the form of:

1. *physical energy*. For example: scrubbing by hand or mechanical equipment. This removes any food debris which may have remained on cooking equipment or utensils
2. *heat energy (thermal)*. For example: hot water or steam. This helps to melt grease and fat, making it easier to scrub clean. Heat energy can also be used to destroy bacteria. This will only happen when the temperature is above 82 °C (180 °F)
3. *chemical energy*. For example: the use of detergents and disinfectants. Note the following:
   - a *detergent* will dissolve grease and fat but will not kill bacteria
   - a *disinfectant* removes infection (reduces bacteria to a safe level) but will not dissolve fats
   - a *steriliser* will kill all living micro-organisms
   - a special cleaning product called a *sanitiser* combines the effects of both detergent and disinfectant.

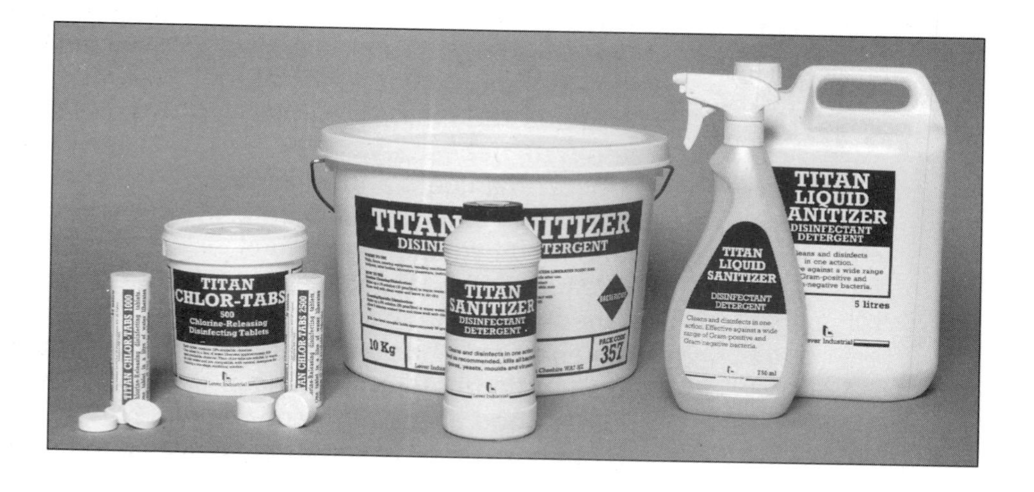

Chemicals used for cleaning

The reasons for cleaning

All food handlers, like doctors, have a *legal and a moral responsibility* to their customers. It is up to you to prevent outbreaks of food poisoning. The reasons we clean are:

- to comply with the law
- to remove any food debris on which bacteria may grow. This will reduce the risk of food poisoning

- to enable disinfectants to be effective on work and equipment surfaces
- to remove any food which may attract food pests, e.g. insects, rodents, birds and domestic pets
- to reduce the contamination of food by foreign matter, e.g. dust, flaking paint, grease from mechanical equipment
- to make the area in which you are working a pleasant and safe place
- to make a favourable impression on customers.

Planning your time

In order to be effective and efficient you need to consider the best method of working, so that cleaning is carried out in a methodical and systematic way.

Replace worn out parts of equipment regularly

- Identify the areas, equipment or utensils that you will be required to clean and when they need to be ready to use again.
- Plan ahead: have all your cleaning equipment and materials ready.
- *Clean as you go* is the basic motto, but always check the most appropriate time to clean.
- Mop up spillages immediately.
- Remember that stoves and floors should be cleaned immediately before and after every service.
- Clean and wipe down walls, shelves, cupboards and drawers regularly.
- Wash out drains and gullies every day.
- Wipe down sinks and hand basins after using them.
- Check cleaning schedules for the best times to clean heavy equipment.

Health, safety and hygiene

Make sure that you are familiar with the general points given in Units G1 and G2 (pages 19–23 and 31–41).

Precautions when using cleaning chemicals

- Always read and follow the instructions carefully. Pay attention to first aid procedures.
- Use protective clothing, e.g. gloves, when handling and using chemicals as some products are highly dangerous when in direct contact with human tissue. Refer to the COSHH regulations (*Control of Substances Hazardous to Health*). Ask your supervisor to supply you with this information.
- Ensure that you use the correct product for the appropriate job, e.g. do not use chlorine bleach on food contact surfaces because it will taint and may contaminate the food.
- Always keep cleaning products in their own containers and make sure they are clearly labelled. Store them in a place which

is not used for food storage.

- *Never* put cleaning chemicals into a food container or food into a chemical container.
- Remember that it is dangerous to mix cleaning chemicals. They may react and give off toxic fumes or they may become ineffective.
- If chemical cleaners require diluting, only do so immediately prior to use; otherwise they may lose their active qualities and become stagnant solutions which may harbour bacteria.
- Always use the correct concentration: if you do not dilute chemical cleaners enough the liquid may be difficult to rinse off and will lead to food contamination; if you dilute them too much they will be ineffective.
- Do not dispose of cleaning solutions in food preparation sinks.
- Clean the cleaning equipment itself (e.g. brushes and cloths) after use. Store them away from food in a well-ventilated area to allow them to dry.

Unexpected situations

If food becomes contaminated with a cleaning chemical it must be discarded immediately. Any spillages of concentrated cleaning chemicals must be carefully diluted and mopped up because they can seriously damage surfaces and equipment.

To do

- Check which cleaning chemicals are used in your kitchen. Read their instructions.
- Note where they are stored.
- Find out what protective clothing/equipment, if any, you need to use when applying each product.

ELEMENT 1: Cleaning food production areas

Areas to be cleaned will include:

- *metal tables, sinks and panelling.* Use a non-abrasive cloth and cleaner. Clean with a detergent and disinfectant, or a sanitiser, then rinse with hot water. Avoid using chlorine bleach or scented disinfectants on food-contact surfaces. Make sure that sinks and hand-basins are clean and free-flowing.
- *wall tiles.* Clean with a detergent and disinfectant, or a sanitiser. Pay special attention to walls around stoves, bins and preparation areas.
- *painted surfaces.* Use a non-abrasive cloth and cleaner. Clean with a detergent and disinfectant, or a sanitiser.

- *floor tiles, vinyl, linoleum floor coverings.* Use a strong degreaser (a detergent) and disinfectant. Ensure that drains, gullies, traps and overflows are clean and free-flowing. While cleaning floors, place an obvious warning sign in the area, indicating that the floor is wet, then dry floors after cleaning to avoid accidents.

A cleaning trolley carrying equipment and warning signs

- *glass.* Use detergent or specialised products. Dry with a clean, soft cloth.
- *laminated surfaces (formica).* Clean with a detergent and disinfectant, or a sanitiser. Make sure that shelving, cupboards and drawers are clean and tidy.

Removing waste

Waste includes all packaging, food trimmings and any leftover food. Waste bins are a perfect environment for promoting the growth of bacteria and need to be treated as a major source of contamination. *Never use a waste bin for storing food* and never use food storage containers (like flour bins) as waste bins.

Follow the guidelines given below:
- empty bins regularly: do not wait until they are full, especially when they contain moist food debris as this will attract pests and bad odours
- take special care after handling rubbish bins and waste food: always wash your hands
- waste bins, their lids and surrounding areas must be thoroughly cleaned. Use a strong detergent and disinfectant
- store waste in the correct designated areas. These should be away from food preparation areas, corridors and fire exits.

Essential knowledge

When cleaning food production areas, waste must be handled and disposed of correctly in order to:
- prevent accidents
- prevent infection from waste
- avoid creating a fire hazard
- prevent pest infestation
- avoid pollution of the environment
- comply with the law.

To do

With guidance from your supervisor, clean:
- metal sinks (checking that they are free-flowing)
- wall tiles (including those around stoves, bins and preparations areas)
- glass surfaces
- the kitchen floor (checking that drains, gullies, traps and overflows are clean and free-flowing)
- any glass surfaces in the kitchen.

What have you learned?

1 Why is it important to handle and dispose of waste correctly when cleaning food production areas?

2 What must you take into account when planning your cleaning?

3 What are the four types of chemicals commonly used for cleaning food production areas?

4 When might you need to use protective clothing when cleaning?

ELEMENT 2: Cleaning food production equipment

Before cleaning

Always make sure that the food production equipment is correctly turned off and dismantled before cleaning. After you have cleaned it, make sure that all the parts are dry and then carefully reassemble the equipment.

See also: *Cleaning cutting equipment* on pages 111–18.

Essential knowledge

All equipment must be turned off and dismantled before cleaning in order to:
- avoid injury to the person cleaning the machine
- ensure that all the relevant parts are thoroughly cleaned
- ensure that the machine works efficiently
- conserve energy.

Cleaning different types of equipment

Ovens

- Use specialised chemicals such as heavy-duty oven cleaners. Pay attention to instructions and take appropriate safety precautions.
- As oven cleaners are highly toxic, ensure that the oven is *thoroughly rinsed* after cleaning.

Griddles or grills and salamanders

- Use specialised chemicals designed to remove carbon (burnt food residues).
- Pay attention to instructions on the packaging and take appropriate safety precautions.

Hobs and range

- Refer to the cleaning manual for the particular equipment you are using, i.e. metal or ceramic, electric or gas-fuelled hobs.
- Ensure that the cooking equipment is isolated from the mains supply before cleaning.
- Correctly re-assemble equipment after cleaning and check that it is operational again.

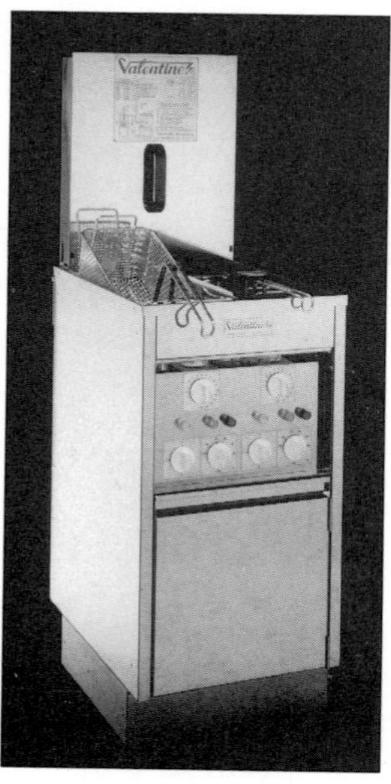
A deep fat fryer

Fryers

Refer to the cleaning manual and use a special degreaser. Take appropriate safety precautions.

1 Ensure that the electricity or gas burner and pilot are turned off.
2 Drain out the oil, using a filter, when the oil is warm; *never when it is hot.*
3 Always drain into a dry, clean container which is large enough to hold the oil easily.
4 Remove the bottom strainer from the fryer and wash this separately with a detergent/degreaser. Dry thoroughly.
5 Clean out any loose scraps of burnt food debris from the fryer. Wash the inside of the pan using a strong detergent/degreaser. Rinse well and dry thoroughly.
6 Clean the lid, the outside of the fryer and the surrounding area, checking for oil spillages.
7 See that the drain tap is closed, and then refill the fryer with clean, strained or new oil.
8 When not in use, close the lid of the fryer, and check that all gas taps are closed and that the mains switch is in the *off* position.

Bain maries or hotplates

- *Dry bain maries:* isolate dry bain maries and hotplates before cleaning and allow to cool. Remove any food debris and clean with detergent and a damp cloth.
- *Wet bain maries:* drain and clean these with a detergent, then rinse them and refill with fresh water.

Refrigerators, freezers and cold rooms

This storage equipment needs special attention.

- Clean the inside walls and floors frequently.
- Mop up any spillages immediately, as they may cause serious cross-contamination.
- Use a detergent and disinfectant which will not taint the food. Rinse very well with hot water.
- Defrost the cooling element regularly. This will prevent a build up of ice and make the equipment easier to clean.
- Plan your cleaning time carefully to prevent the internal temperature of the equipment rising for too long.

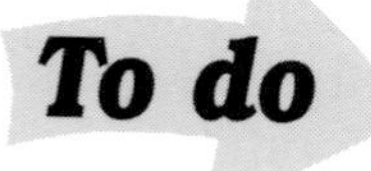

With guidance from your supervisor, clean:

- ovens, hobs and ranges
- grilling equipment, e.g. grill or salamander
- fryers
- dry and wet bain maries
- refrigerators and freezers.

What have you learned?

1 Why is it important to handle and dispose of waste correctly when cleaning food production utensils?

2 Why would you need to use specialised chemicals when cleaning grills and salamanders?

3 How would you clean a dry bain marie?

4 Why must you always turn off and dismantle equipment before cleaning?

5 Why should you regularaly defrost the cooling element of a freezer?

ELEMENT 3: Cleaning food production utensils

All food production utensils need to be kept very clean as they are a major cause of cross-contamination. Make sure they are thoroughly dry before storing them after cleaning.

Stainless steel utensils

This category includes pots, pans and whisks. Clean the utensils with detergents and hot water above 82 °C (180 °F).

Sieves, colanders and strainers may need to be soaked in cold water to loosen the food. The wire mesh of sieves and strainers needs to be thoroughly dried to avoid rust.

Coated metal utensils

Enamel is often used to coat metal utensils, and this can chip very easily. Use a brush or sponge for cleaning, and avoid using abrasive materials and cleaners.

Wood utensils

This category includes spoons and rolling pins. Thoroughly wash these with a detergent and hot water and make sure they are absolutely dry before storing them. Any wooden utensils which have cracks or splinters must be discarded.

Essential knowledge

When cleaning food production utensils, waste must be correctly handled and disposed of in order to:

- prevent accidents
- prevent risk of fire
- prevent contamination of food and food areas
- comply with the law.

Plastic utensils

This category includes spoons, bowls and chopping boards. Thoroughly wash with detergent and a sanitiser, then rinse with hot water (82 °C/180 °F). Take special care when cleaning plastics that cannot withstand extreme temperatures (check the manufacturer's instructions).

Porcelain, earthenware and glass utensils

This category includes bowls and service dishes. Thoroughly wash with detergent and hot water (82 °C/180 °F). Any cracked or chipped utensils must be discarded because they can harbour germs and cause accidents. *Never leave glass items in a full sink.*

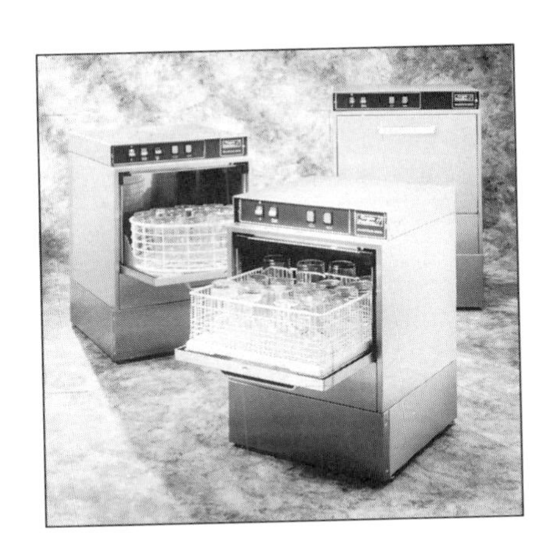

Glasswashers offer a time-saving alternative

Small utensils

These need to be washed with a detergent and hot water (82 °C/180 °F). Make sure that you wash the handles. Knives should be thoroughly cleaned after each use and never left in a full sink. Knives, vegetable peelers and other sharp-edged utensils such as graters need to cleaned and dried carefully to avoid accidents.

Tin openers

These need to cleaned after every use. Use a brush with detergent and hot water (82 °C/180 °F), taking care not to cut yourself on the sharp edge.

To do

With guidance from your supervisor, clean a few articles from each of the following categories:

- stainless steel sieves and colanders
- enamel utensils (if used)
- plastic chopping boards
- porcelain or earthenware service dishes
- knives.

What have you learned?

1 Why must waste be correctly disposed of when cleaning food production utensils?

____

____

____

2 Why should you never leave glass items in a sink?

____

____

3 Why should you check the manufacturer's instructions before cleaning plastic utensils?

---

4 State five precautions that must be observed when using cleaning chemicals.

---

5 What temperature does water need to reach in order to disinfect?

Extend your knowledge

1. Read through the cleaning schedule in your kitchen and discuss the planning of it with your supervisor.
2. Find out exactly how the chemicals in a detergent work.
3. Ask your supervisor for permission to take swab tests from various areas in the kitchen and grow your own colonies of bacteria in a petri dish.
4. Visit a laboratory where food samples from production kitchens are checked.
5. Find out which cleaning agents use an acid base to clean and which use an alkali base.

UNIT 2D17

Cleaning cutting equipment

Element 1: Cleaning cutting equipment

What do you have to do?

- Clean cutting equipment in accordance with laid down procedures using the correct cleaning equipment and materials.
- Dismantle and reassemble cutting equipment correctly.
- Plan your time efficiently and appropriately in order to meet daily schedules.
- Handle, use and store cleaning agents and materials correctly.

What do you need to know?

- The reasons for cleaning cutting equipment.
- How to handle and use cleaning agents.
- The main contamination threats when cleaning.
- How to handle, clean and store cutting equipment correctly.
- How to deal with unexpected situations.

What is *cleaning?*

Cleaning is the removal of all food residues and any dirt or grease that may have become attached to work surfaces, equipment and utensils during the preparation and cooking of food.

To clean effectively, we need to use *energy.* This can be in the form of:

1. *physical energy.* For example: scrubbing by hand or mechanical equipment. This removes any food debris which may have remained on cooking equipment or utensils.
2. *heat energy (thermal).* For example: hot water or steam. This helps to melt grease and fat, making it easier to scrub clean. Heat energy can also be used to destroy bacteria. This will only happen when the temperature is above 82 °C (180 °F).
3. *chemical energy.* For example: the use of detergents and disinfectants. Note the following:
   - a *detergent* will dissolve grease and fat but will not kill bacteria

- a *disinfectant* removes infection (reduces bacteria to a safe level) but will not dissolve fats
- a *steriliser* will kill all living micro-organisms
- a special cleaning product called a *sanitiser* combines the effects of both detergent and disinfectant.

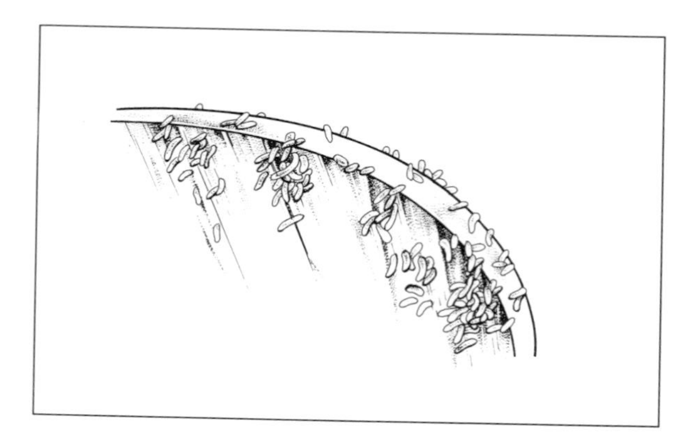

A knife blade that *looks* clean may harbour bacteria visible only under a microscpe

The reasons for cleaning

All food handlers, like doctors, have a *legal and a moral responsibility* to their customers. It is up to you to prevent outbreaks of food poisoning. The reasons we clean are:

- to comply with the law
- to remove any food debris on which bacteria may grow. This will reduce the risk of food poisoning
- to enable disinfectants to be effective on work and equipment surfaces
- to remove any food which may attract food pests, e.g. insects, rodents, birds and domestic pets
- to reduce the contamination of food by foreign matter, e.g. dust, flaking paint, grease from mechanical equipment
- to make the area in which you are working a pleasant and safe place
- to make a favourable impression on customers.

Planning your time

In order to be effective and efficient you need to consider the best method of working, so that cleaning is carried out in a methodical and systematic way.

1 Identify the areas, equipment or utensils that you will be required to clean and when they need to be ready to use again.
2 Plan ahead: have all your cleaning equipment and materials ready.
3 *Clean as you go* is the basic motto, but always check the most appropriate time to clean:
   - mincing machines
   - slicing machines
   - rotary knife (vegetable) chopping machines.

Health, safety and hygiene

Make sure that you are familiar with the general points given in Units G1 and G2 (pages 19–23 and 31–41).

Mechanical cutting equipment is extremely dangerous: every year there are thousands of accidents, some resulting in serious injury and amputation of limbs. The dangers associated with cutting equipment should never be underestimated.

Always ensure that you have been fully trained before cleaning or dismantling any cutting equipment.

Persons under 18 are forbidden by law to clean cutting equipment.

The Prescribed Dangerous Machines Order 1964

This specifies that it is illegal for anyone to operate or clean certain machines unless they have been properly instructed or trained. The following machines fall within this category:

- mincing machines (worm type)
- chopping machines (rotary knife bowl type)
- mixing machines (with attachments for mincing, slicing, shredding, etc.)
- slicing machines (with circular knife)
- potato chipping machines.

All the above mentioned machinery must have clear warning signs stating the danger of the equipment.

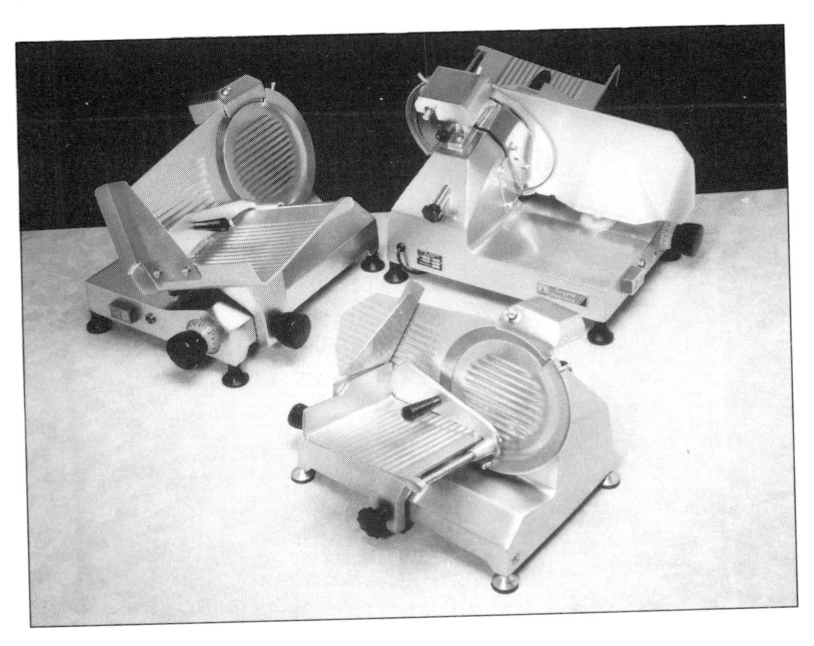

Always ensure that you have been fully trained before cleaning food slicers

To do

- Check which cleaning chemicals are used in your kitchen. Read their instructions.
- Note where they are stored.
- Find out what protective clothing/equipment, if any, you need to use when applying each product.
- Check which items of equipment in your kitchen are listed on the Prescribed Dangerous Machines Order 1964.
- Read the safety notices beside or on the machines. If you cannot find any, report this to your supervisor.

Precautions when using cleaning chemicals

- Always read and follow the instructions carefully. Pay attention to first aid procedures.
- Use protective clothing, e.g. gloves, when handling and using chemicals as some products are highly dangerous when in direct contact with human tissue. Refer to the COSHH regulations (Control of Substances Hazardous to Health). Ask your supervisor to supply you with this information.
- Ensure that you use the correct product for the appropriate job, e.g. do not use chlorine bleach on food contact surfaces because it will taint and may contaminate the food.
- Always keep cleaning products in their own containers and make sure they are clearly labelled. Store them in a place which is not used for food storage.
- Never put cleaning chemicals into a food container or food into a chemical container.
- It is dangerous to mix cleaning chemicals. They may react and give off toxic fumes or they may become ineffective.
- If chemical cleaners require diluting, only do so immediately prior to use; otherwise they may lose their active qualities and become stagnant solutions which may harbour bacteria.
- Always use the correct concentration: if you do not dilute chemical cleaners enough the liquid may be difficult to rinse off and will lead to food contamination; if you dilute them too much they will be ineffective.
- Do not dispose of cleaning solutions in food preparation sinks.
- Clean the cleaning equipment itself (e.g. brushes and cloths) after use. Store them away from food in a well-ventilated area to allow them to dry.

Cleaning cutting equipment

Always refer to the operating manual for the specific details of how to clean the cutting equipment that you use in your kitchen. As a general rule, following the steps given opposite.

1 When you have finished using the machine, *switch it off and remove the plug from the wall socket.* If it is connected directly to a mains unit, isolate it by switching off the electricity supply to the machine.

It is important to isolate the equipment fully so that there is no danger of it being accidently switched on either when the blades are exposed, or when the machine has not been assembled correctly. This could cause serious injury and/or damage to the machine.

When cleaning the equipment you will be using plenty of water and if the machine is still connected to the mains there is risk of an electric shock.

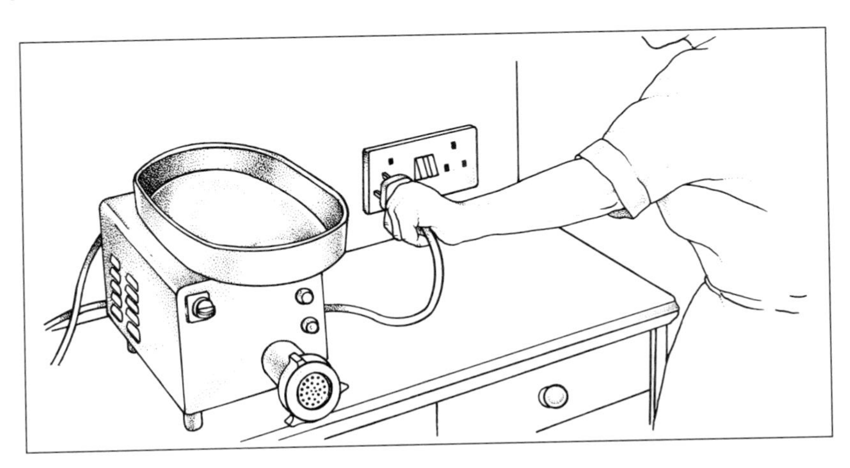

Unplugging a mincing machine before cleaning

2 Carefully remove the guards and any removable parts, e.g. blades, etc.
3 Wash the individual parts in hot detergent water, and dry. *Never leave machinery parts in a sink.*
4 Clean the machine itself, taking care not to use excessive water around the electrical connections.
5 Wash the cutting blades very carefully, using a brush.
6 Check any inside corners for food debris that may have collected.
7 Thoroughly dry the machine and any separate parts.
8 Re-assemble the machine. Make sure that all parts fit correctly and securely.
9 Dry your hands and reconnect the machine to the mains. Switch it on to check that it is functioning correctly.
10 Disconnect from the mains until required.

Essential knowledge

Equipment must be turned off and dismantled before cleaning in order to:

- ensure that parts are cleaned correctly
- prevent injury to the person cleaning
- prevent damage to equipment
- conserve energy.

Points to note when cleaning cutting machines

- Hand-held cutting utensils such as mandolins need to be carefully cleaned with hot detergent water. Use a brush to clean the blade, then rinse clean and dry carefully. Never leave any blades or cutting instruments in a sink.
- Accidents with cutting equipment are caused by carelessness and lack of concentration. In the event of an accident, report it to your supervisor and the on-site first aider immediately (see Unit G1: *Maintaining a safe and secure working environment* (pages 14–18). Apply emergency first aid if you have been trained.

To do

- Make a list of the cutting equipment in your kitchen.
- If you are aged over 18, ask for training in using, dismantling, cleaning and re-assembling the cutting equipment in your kitchen.
- Once you have been trained, clean the cutting equipment in your kitchen.
- Make a note of how to contact your on-site first aider.

What have you learned?

1 List four reasons why we clean cutting equipment.

____

____

____

____

2 Why must equipment be turned off and dismantled before cleaning?

____

____

____

3 Why is it important to plan the time to clean?

____

____

____

____

4 What do you need to check before using a cleaning chemical?

5 Which machines are listed in the Prescribed Dangerous Machines Order 1964?

6 State five precautions to observe when cleaning cutting equipment.

7 What should you do in the event of an accident?

8 Which utensils should never be left in a sink?

Extend your knowledge

1. Research the cases of food poisoning known to have been caused by unhygienic cutting equipment.
2. List the chemical names of substances present in some cleaning agents that may damage cutting equipment.
3. Read through the training guidance notes for all of the dangerous equipment in your workplace.

Index